THE SOUTHERN WAY

CW00481211

CONTENTS

Editorial Introduction	5
North Camp Station: Level Crossing rebuilding, May 1961	6
Boiler Failure on Lord Nelson class locomotive	17
Over the Bridge at Langston	25
The Humble Luggage Label	29
Ashford to Brighton (Via Stoke) Basil K Field, Locomotive Engineer	43
The Southern Traveller's Handbook 1965/66	48
Another Bulleid Enigma	54
Southern Railway Steam Breakdown Cranes. Part 1 - Inherited Cranes	57
South Coast Steam	61
'Rebuilt' - the Letters and Comments pages	73
Generations	78
Terry Cole's Rolling Stock File No. 17	84
The Southern Railway from Inception to Nationalisation. Part 4	87
Paraffin to Coal (via Andover and Salisbury)	101

© Kevin Robertson (Noodle Books) and the various contributors 2012

ISBN 978-1-906419-71-4

First published in 2012 by Kevin Robertson

under the **NOODLE BOOKS** imprint

PO Box 279

Corhampton

SOUTHAMPTON

SO32 3Z

www.noodlebooks.co.uk

editorial@thesouthernway.co.uk

Printed in England by

Ian Allan Printing Ltd

Hersham, Surrey

Publishers note: Every effort has been made to identify and correctly annotate photographic credits. Should an error have occurred then this is entirely unintentional.

ABBAS L.S.W.R^y.

Of course, no sooner had we released the 'Brighton Elevated Electrification' book, than this image of West Croydon arrived. Stephen Grant has kindly provided the following, "Clearances could be tight! By the time the Coulsdon and Wallington scheme went ahead the LBSCR had standardised on a ten inch clearance between the maximum loading gauge height (13ft 6ins above the rail) and any overhead structure such as a bridge, giving a minimum height of 14ft 4ins from rail to bridge. Within this ten-inch headroom, four inches was air clearance between the loading gauge and the underside of the contact wire, two inches was the depth of the 'live construction' (contact wire and supporting catenary) and four inches was air clearance between the top point of the live construction and the overhead structure. This bridge has the necessary ten-inch clearance but, in other instances, a further two inches could be saved by dispensing with the catenary and stretching the contact wire tight between much more substantial supporting ironwork at each end of the bridge. Collector bows on the LBSCR fleet were 3ft wide and curved to follow the contour of the LBSCR's structure gauge, allowing a minimum of four inches vertically and three inches horizontally between any part of the live bow and the structure, after taking into account the rolling movement of the vehicle. The hot, acidic gases from steam locomotive chimneys had a corrosive effect on the overhead construction - the LBSCR found that they had to renew insulators, catenary and contact wire much more frequently on tracks that also carried heavy flows of steam-hauled trains. Also in some locations the ceramic insulators were an irresistible target for stone-throwing youths - some things never change!"

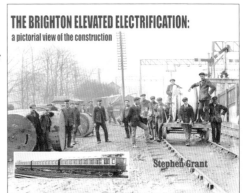

4

Editorial Introduction

Welcome to the latest issue of our periodical. A little bit of catching up has been achieved with this number although I will freely admit I am still embarrassed with the material that sits in a growing pile for inclusion. I do promise we do try to use things in rotation although there is also an attempt to maintain a balance so far as subject matter is concerned.

It will also be obvious from the outset that this particular issue contains a far higher proportion of colour compared with any in the past. For this reason also there is, temporarily, no separate 'Colour Interlude' at the rear, but I sincerely hope the alternatives included will meet with some approval. The change in the balance between colour / b-w for No. 17 has come about because of the importance we attach to the material provided by Colin Martin and his wonderful p/ way slides that form the basis for the lead article. In addition there is Mike Morant's article on luggage labels and Jeffery Grayer's item on advertising. It would be impossible to do these justice without the inclusion of colour. Let me say though that for the present this will not necessarily form the pattern for every issue - I have to raise the spectre of cost again - but I hope an occasional indulgence in these times of austerity might help create a little lift.

Having with this issue also reached 25 issues of 'SW' - including the 'Preview' and seven 'Specials', I am often asked has 'SW' turned out the way I intended? The answer is 'I think so'. I say this because of two particular factors on which I feel as strongly today as I did at the outset. The first is it appears I was not alone in believing there was a need for a Southern-orientated journal - notwithstanding the excellent historical and SR / constituent societies who produce their own magazines for members - but also because I wanted to provide an outlet for the non-mainstream interest. This issue with its features on the slightly off-beat certainly fulfils that criteria.

In one area though I will admit it has perhaps not reached where I felt it might. That is in relation to additional information that might come to light concerning a previously published book but which in itself might not warrant a second or revised edition.

Obviously if that occurs with a book we publish it is an easy matter to slot in an extra page, for often just as something appears in print that elusive photograph appears or the author is contacted by a previously unknown person with the comment, "If you had asked….". All well intended of course.

So, and here I promise I have absolutely no axe to grind with anyone or any publisher, if you have found something new that was omitted from your previous book we are more than happy to include it and give a plug to the original work as well. *(Needs to be SR-related of course!)*

Being fortunate enough also to be able to use this page as a forum for my own personal views and opinions it would be all too tempting to stand on an ever taller soap-box with each edition. I hope I have resisted such temptation so far, but that is about to change. To put matters in context I would first say I recall years ago being frustrated when visiting the then Public Record Office at Kew that we were all ceremoniously turned out at 5.00 pm when I for one would willingly have paid a reasonable fee to continue working into the evening. From speaking to others I understand I was not alone. (Access times have improved since - local record officer please take note!)

But now I turn my attention to Network Rail, not the present day operation but their archive of historic material currently held on an industrial unit 'somewhere around York'. Access to this archive is currently not possible, the organisation citing the comments, 'We do not have the resources available'. They continue that it is the aim for the NRM at York to become the eventual repository for historic plans.

The NRM though state they do not have the resources to administer a large influx of material which then runs the risk of being locked away potentially for a protracted period. Would it then be too much to ask if access might be gained now - not by just turning up, but upon appointment, and even at a charge refundable if an order for copies of plans exceeded a certain amount?

It could even be a means of generating extra income. If you agree you might consider, as I have, dropping them a line with the suggestion.

Kevin Robertson   editorial@thesouthernway.co.uk

Front cover - *Muscle power at North Camp. Colin Martin.*

Rear cover - *Sultry day at Norwood Junction. No. 31064 on shed, 13, July 1957. Norman Simmons*

Pages 2/3 - *Having had locomotive matters as the feature of the initial double-page spread in the past few issues of 'SW', we thought it was about time for a change. Bearing in mind its location it would also have been better in the previous issue on Sam Fay - Itchen Abbas is where he started his railway career - but then this view was located after No. 16 had been published! We see the station viewed towards Alresford, probably in the way Sam would have recognised it, a simple passing place on the line between Alton and Winchester and nearly identical in style to both Alresford and Ropley. Much detail appears in this view that was perhaps unknown at Itchen Abbas previously, the design of telegraph pole, finials on the signal box, and roof chimneys. In the distance there are wagons and a horse-box. One hundred years and more years later everything seen here has ceased to exist.*

NORTH CAMP STATION
Level Crossing Rebuilding: circa May 1961.

Illustrations by Colin Martin
Notes by Graham Hatton

This series of photographs are believed to have been taken in 1961 when alterations to the layout at North Camp station near Aldershot on the SE&CR line from Reading to Guildford were made; and the opportunity was taken to improve the level crossing and the mechanical signalling at this time. They were loaned to the editor by Colin Martin whose father Tom Martin took them whilst engaged in his work here. Tom was in charge of the Guildford relaying gang hence his presence at North Camp. Men from the Raynes Park 'Heavy Renewals' section were also present. They offer a very rare insight into daily engineering work portrayed in colour.

Above - The first view shows the old tarmac crossing and bullhead track at the start of the main work. The Bedford van so typical of many owned by British Railways has brought components and probably towed the compressor sitting beside it to the work site. In the platform is a 'grampus' wagon, again delivering material for the work. Further material and a temporary footbridge, mentioned below, are in the yard beyond it. In the foreground the turnout in the up / down line led to a diamond crossing and on into the yard behind the photographer. This was removed in this work, thus simplifying the rebuilding of the level crossing by reducing the complexity of track passing through the actual level crossing. The trailing slip on the left (of which only its crossing is visible) connected the two running lines and the loop behind the platform where the wagon stands, but it did not connect into the goods yard behind the photographer. In the work being undertaken, these two parallel crossovers were effectively combined into one 'ladder' from the loop line across both main lines to the goods yard. Both diamond crossings in the running line were fitted with slip switches to allow a trailing crossover move in the running lines. Facing slip switches, although not prohibited, are very rare in running lines away from terminal stations as they are considered more of a safety risk.

Top - Any good work starts with a detailed plan and work like this would be supported by drawings for all the elements. These were then tied together and evolved by the Inspector into a work plan. He would also coordinate all the resources necessary and obtain suitable possessions: only then could the actual work start. In order to place items in the new layout a technical surveyor would draw up a general arrangement plan from which the 'signalling' would be able to place their equipment and organise such items as track circuits. As the track layout was

being radically altered this would also include changes to the mechanical locking in the signalling frame as well as the point rodding and its various associated cranks and adjusters. The picture shows a level instrument with the technical staff member reviewing his information. Various other people appear to be readying themselves for a start, but the elderly gentlemen, possibly the Permanent Way Inspector, appears to look as if he has seen it all before, no doubt commenting that they needed to get on. Ultimately though he would know that the technical staff were essential to place the new track accurately ! Note the man with the red flag on the crossing: his presence would indicate that the possession has already been taken and some of the signalling and crossing equipment has already been disconnected.

Right - Large scale mechanisation in engineering is a relatively recent advance. Until around 30 years ago much of the normal relaying was done with basic tools and a lot of muscle. Here the line is starting to be 'opened out'; manually removing the ballast to expose the sleepers and the base they sit on, in preparation for the removal of the old track and in this case much of the crossing construction. Removing ballast below the sleeper level, now commonplace on renewals was not always carried out if it didn't warrant removal.

Depending on the driving concern on the site, which was often just sleeper condition, the old top ballast, was sometimes re-used and simply topped up if its condition was reasonable, some riddling of the ballast being manually carried out to remove a bit of the dirt. In this case however, much of this top ballast is being loaded into the 'grampus' wagon on the left for removal. New ballast will then make up the shortfall. Ballast was removed to a greater extent through the crossing as the new concrete base, seen later, required a greater depth to be removed.

Above - Some time later and still digging! All sites tend to have comedians, indirectly they actually help to break up what was monotonous labour and it looks like someone thinks he has found a ticket to be elsewhere! Various tools are in evidence, a small breaker on the left, picks, shovels and wheelbarrows. On the station it looks like the District Engineer has paid a visit and is standing talking to a member of the station staff. A number of other onlookers are also present, including a man wearing his white motorcycle helmet, the 'corker' style very common at this time with separate goggles. In the corner of the building there are a group of red paraffin road lamps to place on the crossing at night whilst the work continues. Older members of the gangs, often proud of their positions, wear traditional shirts (white!) and ties, even a suit with a flat cap. Younger men wear bib and brace overalls and wellingtons in recognition of the fact this really is dirty work. The men are also using shovels with 'D' rather than a 'T' handle. According to Alan Blackburn, '*No self-respecting Southern man would ever use a 'T' handle shovel.*"

Opposite top - As said in a much earlier article on Lewisham (SW Preview Issue), rest and tea are essential to the progress of physical work. Here men rest briefly on a rail which now forms a convenient seat. Opening out here in readiness for relaying has taken place and more work continues behind, digging out the level crossing base. A tractor and face shovel have arrived to assist in removing material. Work would be divided on site between Permanent Way, Works staff, Mechanical Signalling fitters, etc. Assistance between different work streams was relatively rare, banter was common place. Works staff would do all work in removal of the old level crossing foundation and preparation for the concrete base which was cast over the site later. Use of mechanical breakers fed with compressed air from the compressor on the extreme right would be a works function.

Opposite bottom - Still digging! Below the track now all has been removed in this area: the old crossing surface appear to be deep longitudinal timbers forming a firm base. These were cut with a motorised two-man band saw after the opening out of either side to provide access. Some shuttering has appeared in amongst the men to act as an edge to the concrete base when it is cast. This is Works' staff work: within this staff would be skilled men including carpenters, bricklayers, steel workers etc. A young fireman watches from the platform ramp. One new flat bottom panel of track has appeared in the middle line of platform 2. In order for members of the public to cross the site, who would previously have used the crossing, a small footbridge between the platforms and down into the yard has been erected and a person can be glimpsed using this into the yard with their bicycle.

NORTH CAMP STATION   Level Crossing Rebuilding: circa May 1961

Above - There is a break now between the last and this scene, so this is a following shift after a rest period. The diesel crane is busily assisting the permanent way staff to install the layout. This would first have been pre-assembled elsewhere and then disassembled to leave baseplates fastened to timbers with the rails numbered and marked with paint on the baseplate to aid reassembly. Already the signal department have got in to put the new rodding-run from the signal box 'lead off bed', where rods left the box, across to the new rod run mentioned below and glimpsed behind the pile of timbers. The crane's mess van with facilities to allow the driver probably to live on site with his crane and carry tools to repair any defective parts stands just behind the crane. Note the large size of the goods shed at North Camp with a through line. Sidings in the goods yard were reduced in 1960 and the yard closed in 1969. Quite extensive sidings for war use were put in, in 1941 (lasting largely till 1964) to the west of North Camp with their own signal box known as North Camp Sidings. The track behind the platform was adapted to serve an oil terminal in 1961.

Opposite top - The base of the new crossing has been cast in concrete and from it 'starter bars' stick out to tie the final infill to the base. The new track is laid on timber longitudinal beams with flat bottom running rail and check rails held to base plates with KT clips. The rails are held apart by blocks and bolts as well, the foot of the check rail will have been machined narrower to allow the two rails with their wide foot to sit close enough together. The beams are spaced apart by steel fabricated struts which probably incorporate a threaded bar with nuts on the outside of the bearers to hold them in position. On the left carpenters are fitting spacer blocks between the baseplates and then cutting a capping timber baulk which will sit against the back of both the running and check rail forming a removable edge, to allow access to the permanent way fastenings once the crossing surface is reinstated. These capping timber baulks were held down with vertical bolts, through all the elements, into the longitudinal timbers. The Inspector balances on the centre track, surveying his site.

Opposite bottom - A closer picture of the carpenters cutting notches in the top timber baulks to sit over the baseplates seen between the timber packing pieces on the left-hand rail of the nearer track. On the right-hand rail the top timber baulk has been laid in and shows the top flush with the rail surface. It hasn't yet been bored out to receive the vertical (recessed) bolts to hold it in place. (The position for boring was achieved by the simple means of lifting it over its final position and dropping it. The small indentations left on the underside as a result would then indicate where holes should be drilled.) Although not immediately obvious, this is all hand fettling of the timbers to fit. A lot of the preparation, cutting of timbers, would be done

in a remote workshop in a depot to save time, as the baseplates to take the rail would be spaced on the new timbers to reasonably exact dimensions, but the final fitting would always be a site role. Access to the track fittings is required periodically to ensure the fastenings are indeed holding all the rails firmly and to see if the bolts tying the blocks and rails together need tightening. If the infill material extended up against the running rails or check rails, the material would all need breaking out to allow inspection to happen which would leave a poor, patched crossing surface.

The new track has here been installed with 110A flat bottom rail in inclined baseplates, (where the rails lean towards one another on an inclination of 1:20 to match the coning on the wheels) and fastened down with KT clips and bolts. This view is towards Farnborough North. The single slip in the foreground in the Up line and the next slip beyond in the Down Line allowed movements between the Up and Down lines as a crossover move. They also allow reversing moves from the Up line into the yard, or from the Down line into the bay line behind platform 2. This arrangement of slips where two or more form a long line linking items beyond each slip switch, across other lines, is often referred to as a ladder. These were relatively common as space saving arrangements in terminal stations or complex cramped layouts at this time. This is obviously a small ladder, but some were extensive in length (Eastleigh had one into the yard opposite what was Platform 4): that at Clapham on the Windsor Line side still includes six slip switches of varying type across the three sidings and three running lines it traverses plus the lines at each end which have simple turnouts. The gang on the left are hand sluing the track prior to ballasting. They are being guided by the ganger who is crouching to view the alignment in the Down line slip switches. New point rodding crosses the line in the foreground so sleeper spacing on all lines here would be important to allow straight runs to be workable. In the distance a Drummond engine, probably a 700 goods, is quietly waiting with a mixed freight train.

Above - To the right of the previous photograph, this is a good picture illustrating a number of important items about point rodding set up. As far as possible new rodding runs are straight or follow very flat curves. Less curves means less binding in the rodding. Early rodding used round rods of approximately 1¼ ″ diameter. New rodding used a hollow channel rodding of 1⅝ ″ x 1⅛″which was also galvanised. Rollers in the stools (the support stands) run in this channel under the rodding. The stools are fixed, in this case to concrete trestle supports buried in the ground. Where more acute angles had to be made, various cranks, as shown in the foreground, were used to change abruptly the rodding direction. This rod run has been completely renewed; some old round rods lie to the right. It linked across all the tracks to the signal box on the other side, by rods working various cranks seen disappearing into the timbers of the pointwork. Also coming through from the signal box in the same area are the signal operating wires which pass round the pulley wheels mounted on a large baseplate.

A string line would be used to set the concrete bases to a line which would be established at a constant level or gradient. Then the stools would be fixed on the top and finally the rods run through and their sections fishplated together. This again is specialist signalling fitter work. The mechanical rodding would also be planned carefully as it needed to: a) run in straight lines as far as possible; b) be fitted with compensator cranks to deal with expansion equally on either side of them; c) be able

to be added to, as in the foreground; d) work items in a logical manner - so rods didn't have to have undue cranks added - and of course operate in the appropriate direction when they arrived at the item to be worked. Various 'bottle' adjusters were also incorporated to allow fine adjustment in the rodding when setting up points and other items. Rods also had to be carefully passed under rails which were track-circuited to avoid unnecessary short circuits. Cranks would be formed in the rodding to allow items at different levels to be joined. So much of this mechanical signal work incorporated 'blacksmith technology'. In order to achieve this most of the older signal fitter depots had the facility of forges and blacksmith equipment to allow 'setting' of rods as well as the ability to weld to the ends of rods etc. so as to enable the various permutations to be made. **Right** - removal of the old point rodding.

Above - Mechanised plant! A small tipper wagon tows the concrete mixer away from the site at the end of the work. Again the changes in work wear even over a relatively short period are noticeable. This man is wearing a collar and tie on site, quite common at this time particularly amongst men of any substantive grade. The signals are cleared off which might mean a train is signalled though the site, although during the work of this nature when the locking has been disarranged, signal function would also need testing at the completion of the work, without necessarily indicating a passing train.

Opposite top - The driver of Drummond 700 class No. 30700 looks out cautiously as he traverses the new layout which is still at this stage devoid of top ballast (that between the sleepers as opposed to that below - usually referred to as bottom ballast). Timber numbers can been seen in a few places painted on the timber ends, also some rail paint marks to indicate positioning of rails whilst rebuilding on site.

Opposite bottom - Almost the final job! A Bedford artic, tractor and milk float trailer ('Scammell coupled') for the Home Counties Dairies traverses the new crossing. (How motor vehicle and food technology has changed as well: the lack of a windscreen wiper on the passenger side is an example, whilst milk today is nowadays moved in refrigerated vehicles and no longer in glass bottles.) The bottom track, the Down Main, is complete and the baulk timbers either side of the running rails and check rails can be seen fastened down and the level crossing surface made up to their back edge. It's not clear why the Up Main and siding behind platform 2 has not been quite finished on the level crossing in the same way, prior to completing the main work, but perhaps time did not allow the baulk timbers to be all cut to fit and this was to be completed in a following shift. A timber board has been used at the back edge of where each timber would fit against the road surface and the gap infilled with ballast, which would certainly suggest more work to follow, perhaps in the following weeks. Some infill would appear to have been put on top of the stone strips, in the way of tarmac visible to the right of the lorry to improve this strip area. Without this extra finish it would have left a poor top across the crossing until the work was finished and perhaps that is why the lorry driver's mate is looking out with interest at what has happened. The work can only just have finished as a man appears to be following the lorry with a broom and material still lies scattered around the yard still. The point rodding, although not featured in any of the views, would have passed below the crossing in a specially constructed rod run. This would have required access at frequent locations across the crossing to allow maintenance of the stool rollers, etc.

NORTH CAMP STATION   Level Crossing Rebuilding: circa May 1961

- more from this remarkable series will feature in a future issue.

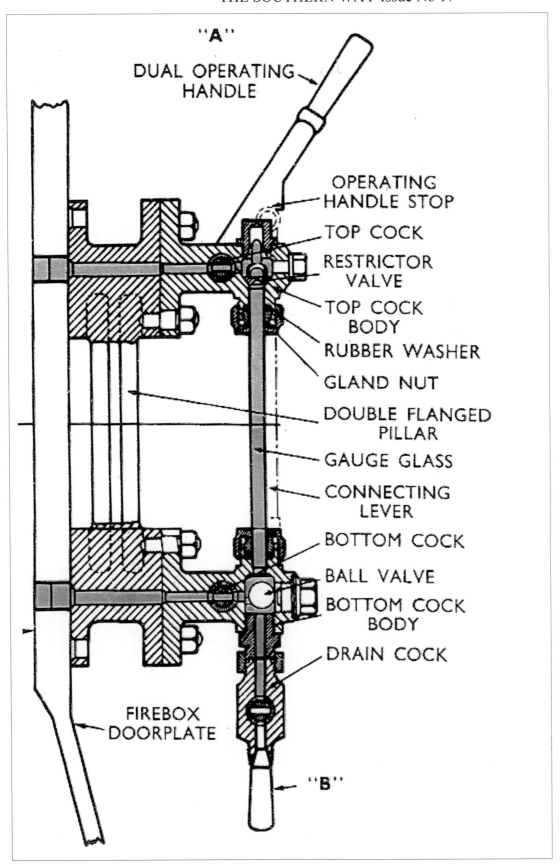

"A"

DUAL OPERATING HANDLE

OPERATING HANDLE STOP

TOP COCK

RESTRICTOR VALVE

TOP COCK BODY

RUBBER WASHER

GLAND NUT

DOUBLE FLANGED PILLAR

GAUGE GLASS

CONNECTING LEVER

BOTTOM COCK

BALL VALVE

BOTTOM COCK BODY

DRAIN COCK

FIREBOX DOORPLATE

"B"

BOILER FAILURE ON LORD NELSON CLASS LOCOMOTIVE

MARTIN BREAKSPEAR

Whenever I have a novice on the footplate at Didcot, I always tell them that the one thing that will save their life is water. Water in the boiler, enough to keep the firebox crown fully covered.

Boiler explosions were fairly common in the early days of steam power. Indeed, the current regulation of steam boilers has developed from the early 19th century toll of lost life and treasure in boiler failures, and initially stemmed from the insurers of industrial plant demanding that the design and in service inspections of boilers be to certain standards to control the insurers' risks and hence loss of profit. Eventually, legislation was brought in and has led directly to today's Pressure Systems Regulations.

The railway companies were both builders and users of steam boilers, and therefore themselves quickly developed standards of design, maintenance and operation. Never the less, boiler failures still occurred from a variety of reasons, from the design-led failure of the LMS ultra high pressure Royal Scot experiment, to poor maintenance as happened to a LNWR loco when the front tube plate failed having corroded away to wafer thin thickness, to poor operational control when the fireman unusually allowed the water level to fall below the level of the firebox crown, leading to its total collapse. It is the failure to manage the boiler correctly that interests in this article.

To control the water level, the footplate crew need to be able to measure the level of water in the boiler. The glass water gauge became the almost universal method of doing this, having been installed for the first time in 1829 by a John Rastrick at his Stourbridge locomotive works. The GWR, for reasons lost in time, stuck to one water gauge with two gauge cocks as back up should the glass gauge fail. More usually, the other railway companies used two glass gauges, placed either side of the boiler back head.

The glass water gauge is a glass tube connected between the boiler water/steam spaces so that the water level can be easily judged in relation to the firebox crown. The illustration opposite shows the usual arrangement locomotives in existence today. Some trade-built smaller locomotives have had a similar arrangement, but the top and bottom boiler passageway cocks are more usually interconnected on company-built engines so that they work together.

The correct operation of the gauge is essential to ensure that it is fully connected to the water/steam space top and bottom, and that the glass is not choked. The total loss system that locomotive boilers operate on means the impurities in the water become concentrated as the steam is drawn off through the cylinders and exhausted to atmosphere. This is overcome by blowing down the boiler, that is, drawing the contaminated water off by opening a valve in the bottom of the water space when the boiler is in steam, and by regularly washing the boiler out when out of service to remove accu-

Left - The Water Gauge, the KEY safety device. Reading the level needs care as going uphill and down dale alters the reading as the water surges. Proving the gauge is fully connected to the boiler is most important.

Right - Sister engine to No. 854, No 30860 'Lord Hawke' at Waterloo on 5 April 1957.
Norman Simmons

(Plenty more images of this type from Norman Simmons to come....!)

mulated scale and sludge. This contaminating material can block up passage ways and valves, and can easily block up the glass gauge so that it does not give a true indication of the water level.

When the top and bottom cocks are interconnected, they should be arranged so that the bottom one opens just before that top one so that the proving sequence can be followed. Without that sequence, the gauge cannot really be proved to be giving a true indication of water level in the boiler.

The fireman must ensure that the gauge glass is giving a true reading of the water level. When first getting on the footplate, the first thing a good fireman will do is to prove the gauge. The correct method for doing this is as follows when there is pressure in the boiler.

The fireman shuts the gauge off by closing both top and bottom cocks. On most locomotives when the top and bottom valves are interconnected, this means pulling just one lever fully down. The gauge is then drained by means of the drain cock, and the water is observed to drain from the glass.

The drain cock is next fully shut, and the bottom (water space) cock is opened very slowly. The water will be observed to slowly move back up into the glass until it stops at a level. This level is **NOT** the boiler water level. What has happened is that the air in the glass has now been compressed up to the pressure in the boiler. The indicated level is now higher than the boiler water level, but what is key is that the bottom of the glass is definitely proved to be connected to the boiler water space, otherwise it could not have let the water in.

Once that is proved, the top (steam space) cock is slowly opened, and the level in the glass should be seen to drop slightly. This happens because the compressed air in the glass is released into the boiler and the gauge water level is now in equilibrium with the boiler. The top cock is now proved to be connected to the boiler steam space.

One final check needs to be performed during operation, and that is the gauge is blown down regularly, every hour say, by just opening the drain cock and observing that the gauge water is blown through the glass. This ensures that the gauge has not become blocked during the run. Remember, this gauge is the only thing that tells you what the water level is in the boiler, and water saves your life!

Some other points should be noted. Once the glass is drained it starts to cool. At 200psi the water is at 200^0C, and hot water entering the gauge will shock a cold glass. Glass does not like shocks. When blowing the glass down, the drain cock should be opened and closed slowly. When firemen blast water through the glass, as some do, the glass is eroded by the steam stream, and I have seen glasses so badly grooved that failure is inevitable. Both poor operational practises will lead to premature glass failure, and having a glass break under even 160psi of steam is dramatic.

Of course, the fireman needs the wherewithal of putting water in the boiler to maintain the level. Water in the tanks, injectors or pumps, and enough boiler pressure to make it work, but that is the subject of another article if the editor agrees.

From above it should be possible for the fireman to always know what the boiler level is, and ensure that danger is avoided, but things do go wrong and failures did occur.

On 23rd April 1945, 'Lord Nelson' class express engine number 854 of Bournemouth shed was rostered to take the 11:02am Bournemouth West to Waterloo. From the subsequent Board of Tarde report, we are told that previously that day the engine had been prepared by Driver Rabbets of Bournemouth shed and completed a five hour turn to Wimborne with Driver Rabbets and Fireman Robbins on the footplate. Fireman Robbins had only two years experienced as a fireman, and but for the war causing labour shortages, would probably still only been doing goods turns if that. He was not Driver Rabbets' regular fireman.

The locomotive arrived at Bournemouth West at 10:00am, and was put on the Waterloo coaches at 10:45am. From their evidence, the fireman had the injector on, and when he shut it off, Driver Rabbets noticed that he could not see the water in the gauges. The fireman assured him that it was in the "top nut", meaning that the water level was above the top of the glass. Rabbets claimed that he satisfied himself that this was the case by draining a gauge down and witnessing the water drain down, and then rise up again out of sight. After leaving Bournemouth West, he noticed the water level showing in the top of the glass when going up the steep incline before joining the main Dorchester-Bournemouth line. This might seem a bit odd in that going uphill, the water would run towards the backhead and make it seem that the boiler was fuller than it actually was. Yet Driver Rabbets says that it was in the top nut at Bournemouth West. The injector was put on, and the water quickly disappeared above the top nut where it remained until they reached Bournemouth Central. At the Central station, the crew handed the engine over to Driver F Billett and Fireman V J C Perry. Fireman Perry was also a passed driver, and had been Driver Billett's regular fireman for 18 months, and was therefore a well-qualified and experienced man on the shovel. At that time, the boiler had a full head of steam and supposedly a very full boiler.

For some reason there does not appear to have much of a hand-over at Central station, the crew just exchanged. However, Driver Billett later admitted that he could not see that the top of the water in the gauges and assumed that it was in the top nut. It appears that this was in fact usually the case, probably because coming out of West Station it was the practice to have the boiler full and up to pressure ready for the London run. Driver Billett admitted that he did not try the gauge cocks himself, nor did he witness Fireman Perry doing so until they were ½ mile from Central Station. Driver Billett said later that the injector on Fireman Perry's side was used freely up the bank from Christchurch, and pressure was easily maintained. About 1 ½ miles short of New Milton, Driver Billett heard a noise and remarked that the safety valves were going to lift, but Fireman Perry countered that stating that the pressure gauge was only reading 210 lbs per sq inch, 10 lbs per sq inch below the safe working pressure. Driver Billet tried to locate the sound, and concluded it was coming from the fire box. He stated he then observed the water to be within 1 inch of the top of the gauge. He decided to defer examination of the gauge until the New Milton Stop. A moment later, the firebox crown collapsed.

Fireman Perry must have been standing in front of the firebox doors. Even if they were shut, the force of the boiler water being ejected into the firebox and flashing off as superheated steam would have been huge, and a blast of hot combustion gases and steam would have been forced into the cab. Fireman Perry was badly scalded and burned. Driver Billett managed to evacuate the cab receiving minor burns to hands, wrists and neck. From outside of the cab he reached back into the cab to apply the brakes and bringing the train safely to a halt in about 1000 yards. Help was immediately given by two American and one British doctor, but to no avail for Fireman Perry. He died in hospital some three days later from his injuries. The train was delayed some 78 minutes whilst a pilot engine was arranged, and the necessary wrong line signalling arrangements made to get it on to the train. Such a speedy resumption of service would be most unlikely today with the excruciating Health and Safety input.

THE BOARD OF TRADE REPORT

The accident was investigated by Mr J L M Moore of the Board of Trade railway inspectorate division. His report detailed the full circumstances of the accident, and comes to some very critical conclusions for all 4 footplate staff.

The boiler and firebox General Arrangement drawings below and overleaf (GA) will aid understanding of the design

The 'Nelson' class of engine has a copper firebox 10 ft 6 inches long by 3ft 4 1/4inches wide towards the top, being a Belpaire design. The wrapper is a single sheet, $^{9}/_{16}$ inch thick, riveted to a $^{5}/_{8}$ inch thick tube plate. The crown slopes back towards the cab, being 3 inches higher at the front. There are 360 direct roof stays, protected from the fire by 1 inch full nuts.

The crown of the firebox is fitted with 3 fusible plugs. The fusible plug is a supposed safety device, essentially a hollow steel bolt filled with lead. Its purpose is to melt the lead out should the crown become overheated before the main structure becomes seriously weakened. The resulting small hole in the plug allows steam to blow into the firebox, alerting the crew by the noise and providing some cooling effect on the fire. The drawing on page 21 illustrates what the plug looks like.

The plugs are fitted along the longitudinal centre

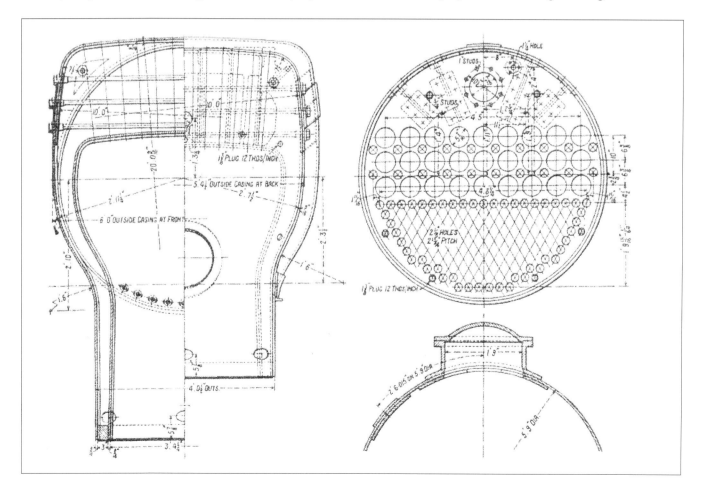

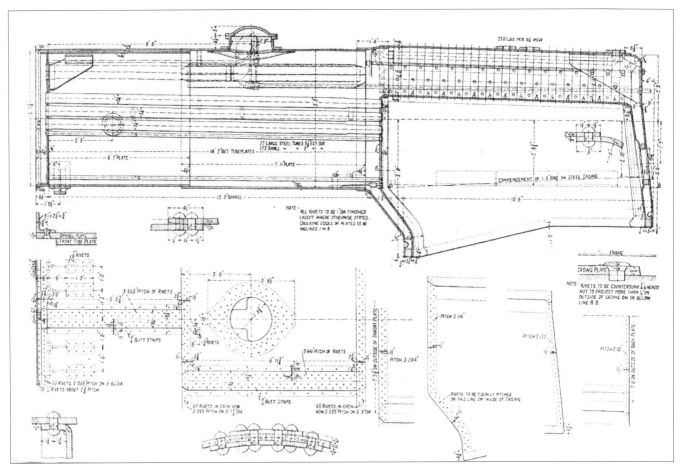

line of the crown, 8 inches and 16 inches from the tube plate, and 8 inches from the backhead, referred to in the report as the front, middle and back plugs. Each plug is 2 $\frac{11}{16}$ inches long, projecting into the water space by about 1 inch. The plugs are filled with 99.75% pure lead, and fill the top 1 $\frac{1}{8}$inch of the plug. These details are important in Mr Moore's conclusions as to why so little warning about the imminent failure was provided by the plugs melting.

The engine left Eastleigh works on March 20 1945 after a general repair, and had run 6,300 miles prior to the accident. It was a Bournemouth shed engine. The boiler was last examined on April 18 by the shed leading boiler smith when the boiler was washed out, five days before the accident. He reported that all was in order, including the water gauge frames. He was again in the firebox on April 22 to deal with some leaky tubes. He made a superficial examination of the fire box at that time. He would have looked at the fusible plugs, and found everything in order. A full exam would have included checking the stays, seams and fittings, the work on April 22 would have been in the nature of running repairs. Like any good craftsman, he would have cast his eye around the box to check that there were no obvious signs of trouble. Any incipient bulging of the plate work would have been obvious at once, and lead to an immediate failure of the engine. We may presume therefore that the firebox was in good working condition at that time.

After the accident, a well-defined mark was found along the tube plate and sides of the firebox indicating that the water level had been at least 3 inches below the highest point of the crown at the firebox front. Above that mark, the plates were badly discoloured by scorching. The crown plate was bulged downwards by 18 inches at the lowest point, with 196 nuts forced off the stays, and a further 27 others showing signs of distortion. Of the 30 transverse stays seven at the back of the firebox remained intact, and only one at the front. There was a tear in the crown 18 inches long, towards the back of the bulge, and other damage indicating severe shortage of water.

The lead in the middle fusible plug had completely melted, and only a small amount remained in the front plug. The back plug had significantly more, but would still have allowed steam to pass.

There was other damage to the fire doors, smoke box doors and other fittings. However, and most importantly, the gauge fittings, safety valves and pressure gauge were found to be still in perfect working order, with the pressure gauge accurate to calibration. The injectors were also proved to be working normally on test.

The damage indicates the size of the forces involved. The pressure on the firebox crown even at 10 lbs per square inch below safe working pressure means that some 715 tons were pressing down on the crown overall. To tear 196 1 inch nuts off in an instant takes some doing. Damage to other items like the smoke box door would have been caused by the sudden over pressure in the firebox.

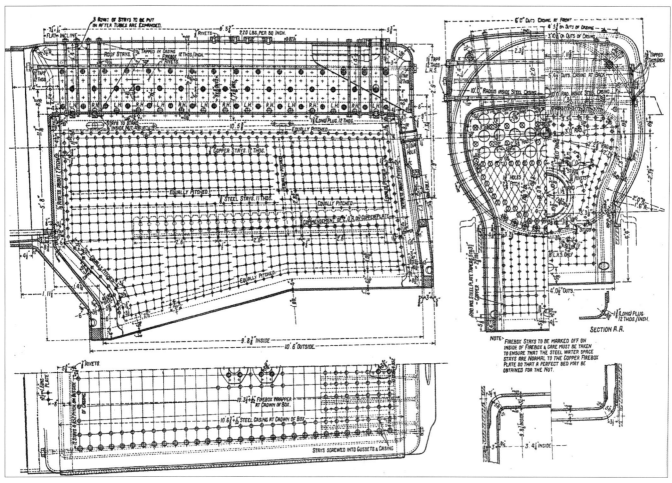

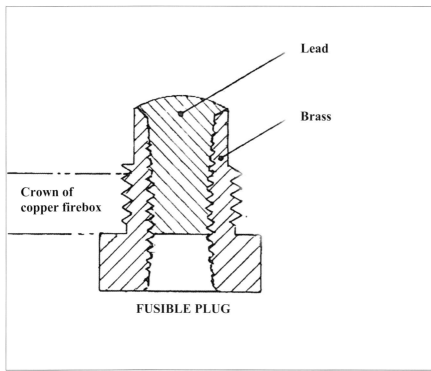

FUSIBLE PLUG

Lead

Brass

Crown of copper firebox

BOILER GAs - *These are the drawings from which the boiler was built. The fusible plus can be discerned on the firebox crown. There are two very near the front of the firebox, and one towards the rear. As can be seen, due to the slope of the crown, the rear one is a lot lower than the front two.*

FUSIBLE PLUG - *The fusible plug is a large hollow bolt, filled with low melting point lead. Under normal operation the water (even though boiling at $200^0 c$), keeps it cool enough for the lead not to melt.*

The picture show a gauge with 1/3 glass, with the back ground hatching clearly being refracted differently where the water is. This considerably aids reading the gauge, especially when the water is out of sight.

Remember that the water at 200^0C would have flashed off immediately into steam, and one gallon of water makes 1746-odd gallons of steam, all trying to get out of the fire box, The explosion would have been violent and instantaneous. Not a pleasant experience. Driver Billett did well to keep his head and apply the brakes to bring the train to a stand.

Mr Moore concluded that the water level must have been out of sight below the lower gauge nut before the train left Bournemouth West, and possibly earlier. When the engine is standing on level track, this nut is only $^7/_8$ inch above the highest fusible plug, and probably the latter was only intermittently covered by the water from the early stages of the journey.

Mr Moore calculated that had the water been above the top nut when leaving West station, the engine could have travelled well beyond Milton even if no further water had been added to the boiler; indeed, it might have gone a further five miles before the crown became uncovered sufficiently to collapse in the way that it did.

It was an easy (and indeed in my opinion, an essential) matter to test the gauge when the Waterloo-bound crew took over the engine at Central station. This is even more so a required duty as the water level could not be seen. In failing to do so, Driver Billett placed too much reliance on others. As the driver, he was fully responsible for all footplate actions and for supervising the fireman, even though in this case Fireman Perry was well qualified. He might not have expected that Driver Rabbets, let alone Fireman Robbins, to have made such a fundamental and dangerous mistake as to allow the water to get so low, but even so, he was not justified in placing such reliance on them. Fireman Perry himself appears to have relied on the previous crew's good management of the boiler, and in doing so, lost his life. In the end however, it was Driver Billett's responsibility and Mr Moore placed the blame squarely on his shoulders.

Mr Moore considered that Driver Rabbets was also culpable, and refused to accept his statements that both he and Fireman Robbins managed the water level correctly. He believed that they paid little or no attention to the gauge glass over a considerable period. It was inexplicable to him how these men allowed the water to disappear below the bottom nut and still believe that all was well. Fireman Robbins admitted to not testing the gauge during the 5 hours he was on the footplate, and there must also be grave doubts that Driver Rabbets did so either. As stated above, the procedure for the initial check is clear, and blow downs every hour or so ensures that the gauge still giving a true reading and the water level is where you want it. Mr Moore concluded that Driver Rabbets who had been a driver at Bournemouth for 25 years, had clearly failed to supervise Fireman Robbins, a man who needed watching.

Mr Moore's report emphasises the uncertainty of the design of fusible plug in giving adequate warning of low water level. As stated above, the purpose is that the lead melts and a jet of steam is projected into the firebox where the noise and visual effects alert that crew that they need to take some prompt action.

He believed that although the middle plug melted completely, it must have done so within a minute or so of the crown collapsing. The front and middle plugs must have been uncovered for some 7 or 8 minutes at least. There could be no doubt that the lead commenced melting as soon as they became uncovered, the physics demand so. However, the steam leaking past the remaining lead must have had a chilling effect and delayed the lead melting fully out. There would also have been water splashing over the front plug from the remaining water in the boiler barrel which would have been boiling furiously. This would also have delayed the front plug from melting out completely. The back plug, which had the most lead remaining, sat 4 inches lower than the front one, and would have therefore been the last to melt. The crown obviously collapsed before the lead had fully melted out.

To be fully effective, the plug must give unmistakable and timely warning to the crew that something is amiss. This obviously did not happen in this case according to the Driver's evidence to Mr Moore. Mr Moore therefore recommended that the Railway companies reconsider the design of the fusible plugs, as it was common across all company-built engines.

In addition, Mr Moore commented on the need for gauge glasses to be more easily read, especially when the water is out of sight. Water-filled gauge glasses refract (that is, bend) the light differently to empty ones. The simple expedient of placing a white black plate stripped with diagonal black lines behind the glass gives a clear reading, as in the illustration opposite. When the black stripe is reversed, it gives a clear indication that the glass is full of water at that point, and Mr Moore recommended that the companies adopt it.

Although Mr Moore's report must be taken as a true and fair appraisal of the events, there are some discrepancies in the report and maybe some areas of doubt. (A minor error in the sizes of the firebox is clear [not from the text, it isn't – I assume that if one looked at the GA drawings one would see that there was some discrepancy – it might be more helpful if he specified what it was.]) However, Fireman Perry's death deprives us of his evidence, and there is no indication that Mr Moore spoke to him before he died. There is the possibility that the water level was as Driver Billett reported in his evidence, and the damage was caused by Fireman Robbins' negligence. Mr Moore is quite clear that he distrusts Driver Rabbets' and Fireman Robbins' evidence. He says that the range of the engine with a full boiler at Bournemouth would have taken it past New Milton. That may have been true, but if the crown was weakened by Fireman Robbins, then it is possible that it failed with a full boiler. Locomotive boilers are highly stressed pressure vessels, with constant variations in temperature and pressure. Driver Billett says that Fireman Perry reported a pressure of 210 lbs per sq inch just before the crown collapsed. A very weakened and damaged crown may have finally failed during normal and correct operation subsequent to being uncovered. Of course, as soon as the crown went, the only true evidence of the water level at that time disappeared into the firebox. At this point in time, we will never know.

Boiler failures are thankfully rare in this country, and long may that be the case on our heritage railways. We need to be thankful to all of those that give us our steam heritage "in the flesh" as it were. The risk is there however, and only competent maintenance and operation will keep the disaster at bay. That professional enginemen who were doing it every day of their lives could make such a mistake does show however that things do go wrong. This collapse was not the only one. Around this time there were at least two Merchant Navy crown collapses due to low water, thankfully not disastrous because the thermic siphons offered both thermal and structural safety margins, and *Duchess of Atholl* suffered a collapse for the same reason. In the chaos and stress of war there would have been other similar incidents or near misses.

No. 30857 'Lord Howe' shunting at Clapham Junction, 5 April 1954 - the coal seems none the best! Sister engine No. 854 was repaired after the New Milton accident and survived until September 1961. It was cut-up at Eastleigh shortly afterwards. It was unfortunate but on 24 April 1945 the engine had only recently been back in traffic one month following a general repair at Eastleigh. It was to Eastleigh also that is was taken for repairs after the incident. The force of the firebox collapse created enough pressure to blow open the smokebox door which in turn was ripped around deforming the nearside smoke deflector. No. 854 would be involved in another incident a few years later, coming to grief at Shawford when the driver misread a signal.

'OVER THE BRIDGE AT LANGSTON'

No prizes this time for guessing the location: the unmistakable vista of Langston Harbour on the Hayling Island branch with (left) No. 635 taking a train south towards Hayling. No date unfortunately, but with the 'LBSC' insignia displayed we can at least say it should be 'pre-1923'. (One of the highlights has to be the silhouettes of the passengers, especially the lady with the hat in the first coach.) What can be spoken of with more certainty is the little 'Langston Bridge' signal box. Just five levers and as this was a single line bridge with no turnouts to control, it will be gathered was classified as a 'NBP' - non block post. (The 'Signalling Record Society' refer to the five levers although in the Middelton press book on the Hayling branch there is mention of seven levers.) The single line section was from Havant through to Hayling itself, the line being worked on the 'staff and ticket' principal from at least 1884 onwards and possible, even from the time of opening in 1865.

The purpose of the signal box was simply to control stop signals (and bolt locks) protecting the swing-portion of the bridge (the engine is on the actual swinging portion), the latter aspect hand-operated. Up to 1938 the signal box had been manned on a full-time basis although after this it was a simple 'as-required', with notification made to Havant in advance. Even so it would still be subject to a mutually convenient time. When this agreed time was reached, the railway signals would first be returned to danger and a lengthman would disconnect the fishplates and signal wires. The locking bolts would then be withdrawn by the signalman (also referred to as a 'bridge-man') operating the levers in the signal cabin. The swinging portion of bridge - a 30' span - was then moved by hand by the two railwaymen inserting cranked poles as seen over the page. How regularly this occurred in later years is perhaps questionable - according to Alan Bell it took place just nine times in 1949 and no doubt diminished further in later years.

The structure of Langston Bridge was of all-timber construction, and thus restricted the weights that could be carried, double heading by two 'Terrier's' prohibited. (Fire buckets were contained in huts at either end of the 1000' structure for use in emergency - there is dispute between the two books over the length of the bridge, referred to also as having been 1,100 feet.) At the end of the 1920s major strengthening was carried out on the bridge with concrete supports provided and new timbers. Further investment was required by the early 1960's costed at the time at £400,000 but which would have allowed heavier weights to be carried. Unfortunately the annual operating profit for the railway at just £2,000 was insufficient to warrant such a large outlay. The age of the Terriers', the only type of locomotive able to use the line, was another the reason for closure in 1963.

In the illustrations the permanent way is interesting, clearly chairs are seen in the view lower right, but elsewhere overleaf the track is definitely of the flat-bottom type. Were the views taken as a 'before and after' record with the passage of the vessel conveniently recorded? (The vessel may be 'Langstone', operated a local firm and used for the transportation of aggregate.) The spelling of Langston / Langstone appears to have varied over the years.

"On a vessel approaching the railway-bridge, the bridgeman will hoist on the flagstaff at the centre of the bridge a white flag by day, or a white light at night, to denote that the vessel is seen. If the bridge can be safely opened, a black ball will be hoisted by day and green light by night. When the bridge is actually open, a red flag will be hoisted by day and a red light* by night and shown until the bridge is about to be closed for the passing of trains. Masters and Pilots are not allowed to sail through the opening of the bridge, but must bring their vessels up to the proper mooring buoys provided for that purpose and there remain until the signal is exhibited, as above, that the bridge is open, when they must warp their vessels through".
*owing to lack of use the red lights were abolished in 1950, as they were not a legal requirement.

See also illustrations overleaf

Further reading: *THE HAYLING RAILWAY* - Oakwood Press
BRANCH LINE TO HAYLING - Middleton Press.

LONDON BRIGHTON & SOUTH COAST RAILWAY.

LOOK AFTER

YOUR

LUGGAGE

AND

BEWARE

OF

GAMBLERS

AND

PICKPOCKETS

THE HUMBLE LUGGAGE LABEL
(SOUTHERN 'WAY' OF COURSE)
Mike Morant

The Southern Way's readership is fortunate to have as its Hon. Ed. someone who appreciates the esoteric aspects of railway matters and we are regularly regaled with background on topics which one is unlikely to have come across in the longer established journals. Luggage labels, part and parcel of railway operations for about 110 years, have received short shrift over the years as most mainstream railway archive magazines seem to be obsessed with locomotives and little else. The one exception that I can recall is Back Track which has published at least one illustrated article on pictorial railway labels but that, amongst label collectors, is a category in its own right and is not mentioned again here.

Coverage

This article is intended to describe but a flavour of the variety of luggage labels in the southern parts of England from the 1850s through to post-nationalisation times. An in-depth analysis of the labels from either the LSWR or the SE (C)R isn't possible within the space available but an attempt is made here to summarise the salient points in the phases of development of the genre. Notable by their absence are the Colonel Stephens railways which might disappoint some readers but his undertakings didn't extend to such relative luxury and they were never part of the SR or its constituents in any case.

Background

Luggage labels were free of charge to travellers who transported their luggage unaccompanied and were produced as cheaply as possible for that reason. We would call them disposables in modern accounting parlance but that doesn't imply that they weren't colourful or lacking in aesthetically pleasing appearance. Indeed, the SER, LSWR and IoWR all used coloured paper extensively probably to compensate for illiteracy amongst staff as their labels' colouring schemes were route-oriented but more of that later. The labels were stored in wooden racks with some of those mounted inside booking/parcels offices whilst others were simply attached to walls on sides of station buildings and usually open to the elements which brings us to something that puzzles many people when one mentions that one collects this genre. The assumption for some reason is nearly always that collectors trudge around car boot sales and bric-à-brac shops looking for old suitcases with labels on them. Nothing could be further from the truth as the most sought after are in the condition that they were in when they left the printers no matter how old they are. Of course, that is an ideal that can never be achieved but it would surprise most people who have never seen such a collection just how high the proportion is of nearly mint labels going back over 150 years.

Paper colour has been mentioned above and will be covered in greater detail as we progress but there are other aspects which should be mentioned at this point. The labels were applied to baggage by the relevant railway staff who would have had a small container part-filled with homemade flour paste and a stiff (-ish) paint brush to hand. A small detail worth mentioning is that pre-gummed backs to luggage labels which required only the application of water to become adhesive were commonplace but no railway based south of the Thames/Severn line ever had them.

Little, historically, has survived in print - or been discovered to have survived - on the subject of labels generally but it is known that The Times newspaper published an article in 1845 which hailed them as an ingenious invention (author's *note: my, hasn't the world moved on!*) that will help to prevent the loss of packages in transit but that was describing parcels labels rather than those for luggage.

The Why and the Wherefore

There are many reasons <u>why</u> collectors of paper railwayana have chosen to collect luggage labels:

♦ A specialised interest in a specific railway.

♦ Historical perspective.

♦ An obsession with a specific place or area which amounts to "collect everything come what may".

♦ Not to be discounted is that it's a relatively cheap entry point to railwayana collecting.

♦ Completism which, to this writer's surprise is a real English word albeit in the Oxford Dictionary of Science Fiction but we all know what is meant by it.

The latter is usually a fool's errand simply because previously unknown material comes to light surprisingly frequently.

The <u>wherefore</u> is dependent upon the personal view of the collector and is difficult to define. My own background is in railway photography and collecting paper railwayana would seem to be a world away from that but my introduction to luggage labels harks back to my early days with a camera in about 1956 traipsing around dark and dingy stations with my elders (and betters) hunting down luggage label sources. Sadly, most of the labels accumulated in those early years which included an unencumbered 'raid' on the massive LSWR racks at Waterloo were exchanged for something in about 1968 but I was smart enough to keep the spares which were resurrected in 2000 to form the basis of my collection. The <u>wherefore</u> in my case is that it moved me away from that obsession so many of us have with loco-motives and into a burgeoning interest in stations, their loca-tions and histories.

Which railways and what has survived?

The answer to the first question is a simple one as BR(S), the Southern and all immediate constituents thereof at the 1923 grouping produced large quantities of luggage labels. In addition, the LC&DR and S&DJC used them although the former are in short supply in terms of different destina-tions.

The minor constituents such as the PDSWJR, L&BR and the railways of the Isle of Wight have left us few survivors into the modern era but there are some still in col-lections.

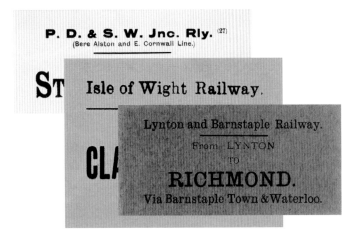

The "survive" word in different forms has already been freely used above and that influences collections as well as collectability. Luggage label collecting, in the formal sense, is a relatively new hobby and the first book on the subject was published in the early 1980s but the hobby embraces over one hundred years of our railway history and that begs the question; how have so many hundreds of thousands, survived? The answer to that probably lies with railway photographers, track-bashers (*sic*) and hoarders in general which, in my experience, applies to just about every trans-port enthusiast I've ever met. The bulk of what is around today was acquired, roughly speaking, from the mid-1950s through to the mid-1960s during which period there was wholesale abandonment of branch lines, other station clo-sures and of course the mass retirement of the older parts of our steam engine fleet. All of that coincided with a growing interest in all of the above plus a burgeoning increase in

enthusiasts' rail tour charters. Participants in those genres were, in many cases, on the *qui vive* for souvenirs and the cheaper the better! What, rhetorically, could be cheaper or easier to help oneself to than luggage labels? The bulk of such acquisitions were simply hoarded and many such accu-mulations survive to this day exactly as they were half a century ago with no heed paid to them by their owners.

However, - there's always one of those isn't there? - there was another informal group of luggage label accu-mulators during that period and they displayed great pre-science because much of what is available today has come to us as a result of their considerable and concentrated ef-forts to preserve as much as possible. They were probably the first serious collectors and went around their own 'patches' or regions acquiring everything they could lay their hands on. It no doubt helped that, amongst the ones I knew personally, they were mostly BR employees with local knowledge and also that BR, like it or not, was in a time warp.

There are many tales both confirmed and apocry-phal about luggage labels in the south and no doubt there are similar stories pertaining to the rest of Britain and Ireland as well.

◆ One such is that BR had a clear out of the cellars at Waterloo station and packing cases containing vast numbers of neatly packaged labels were found. This is almost certainly true many as examples of both SR and LSWR labels with Waterloo as the originating station are rife.

◆ An e-correspondent informed me quite recently that he acquired his LSWR labels (printed on col oured paper and therefore pre-1889) from Frimley station as late as 1972.

◆ There is a tale that by 1952 there wasn't a single pre-grouping label left on the Isle of Wight which, if true, suggests that label collecting goes back fur ther than one might think although one collection was discovered less than five years ago in America of all places that had been compiled as far back as 1875.

There is another side to this coin and it affects collectors to this day. All the writings above refer to what was collected back in the day but there were stations at which the staff guarded their anachronisms with missionary zeal and so, sadly, much of what was there ended up being destroyed when the time for closure or modernisation came around. One such seems to have been Waterloo (East) although the labels correctly referred to it as Waterloo Junction. There are a few survivors from there and so somebody managed to find his way past the Praetorian Guard or, as we would call them today, jobsworths.

Venerable, vulnerable and relative scarcity

A label's age is not a criterion when judging relative scarcity but the well known law of supply and demand is. LBSCR labels from Partridge Green, opened in 1861, mostly as fresh as the day they left the printer, have flooded the market forever and a day but labels, including post-grouping, from the likes of Southampton West are very hard to find.

Vulnerability also affects supply and demand. The plethora of antiques programmes on television continually stress the importance of condition and it's every collector's wish to own as pristine a collection as possible. However, although the earliest labels have survived the ravages of time very well, supposedly because the paper had a high cotton content, labels produced for a lengthy period in the late 19th century were printed on very poor quality paper indeed and the present day collector suffers. Those labels are prone to dessiccation, can crumble to the touch and a particular example of this phenomenon is apparent with the labels from Waterloo to the Isle of Wight, resulting in some of them being very scarce indeed. Another factor that has led to fragility is that label racks were often open to the elements which has led to the contents becoming weathered and brittle.

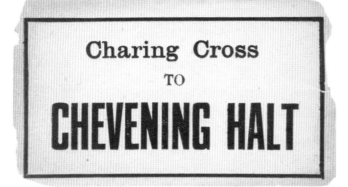

The topic of relative scarcity is interesting in itself in the main because what may be perceived as a criterion is actually the opposite of what one might expect. Some label sellers who use a well known internet auction site to advertise their wares stress the fact that the labels are "to closed stations" which, on the face of it, suggests scarcity: but the opposite is far more likely to be the case, as it is the early printings of labels to the busier stations that haven't survived simply because they were all used and were subsequently replaced by newer versions.

What's in a name?

Luggage labels are traditionally thought of as oblong or square pieces of paper with the issuing company's title at the top and the destination station occupying the central part of the label, perhaps with routing information in smaller print below that. What might be considered odd is that very few railways' labels ever actually mention the words 'passenger' or 'luggage'. Indeed, neither the SR nor any of its constituents did so with the inevitable exception of what is referred to as 'the blank' ~ a misnomer if ever there was one ~ but that will be described later.

Mention has already been made above of "the familiar face of luggage labels" but it isn't quite as straightforward as it seems to be. The SER/SECR, with the exception of a few labels titled the "S. E. & C. & D. Railways" and labels connected with European travel, never displayed the issuing company's name on its labels and this policy continued briefly even into post-grouping times. With but a few exceptions the normal heading was a single title line proclaiming the railway's name in full or nearly so. However, the earliest format of LBSCR labels is inconsistent, with some sporting a single and very neat title line whilst others have the title spread over two lines with variations as to where the division of text is made. Some are even expressed in italic form which is very unusual.

> London Brighton and South Coast Railway
>
> London Brighton and South Coast Railway.
>
> *London Brighton and South Coast Railway.*
>
> *Ford to*
>
> **Portslade.**

With the exception of but one printing style which is spread over two lines, the LSWR maintained a consistent single line policy for the company's title.

The major exceptions to the single line title lie with the P.D. & S.W.J.R. which proclaims that it is the "Bere Alston and E. Cornwall Line" whilst the ever popular S. & D. has as its first line a proclamation of ownership followed by the sub-title "Som. and Dor. Joint Line" or variants thereof.

Halt! Who goes there?

Who, indeed? The SECR was prolific in its provision of labels to halts whilst the Southern continued that tradition on a lesser scale after the 1923 grouping. Elsewhere the opposite was true with none on either the minor SR constitu-

THE SOUTH EASTERN CORNER

The Southern and most of its constituents are pictorially well represented within the text part of this article but the SER/SECR/LCDR are barely to be seen and so these pages redress the balance somewhat. As will be seen, the SER/SECR labels were devoid of a company title but the sheer variety of style and colour fascinates many an ardent collector. These images are all displayed at approximately 66% of their actual size.

SECR hop pickers' label. Note that all the hop-pickers labels have an accentuated first letter.

Southern transitional hop pickers' label. No railway title as yet but the printing date has arrived.

The Southern version with title line and printing date.

A typical example of an SECR label to a 'foreign' destination.

SECR label.

One of the attractive diagonal prints to Charing Cross.

The tan coloured was used for the Caterham and Tattenham Corner branches but the diamond frame was for the former only.

The SECR was generous with its attribution of halts with this one being a prime example.

One of the few mentions of the Chatham & Dover on an SECR label.

One of the few mentions of the Chatham & Dover on an SECR label.

SECR label.

An example of the garish diagonal prints to Cannon Street. The backs of these labels are actually white.

Not only is this label aesthetically pleasing and very rare but the journey for the luggage is mind-boggling for the era when it was printed.

Variety is the spice of life. This is the design for SE(C)R labels for the Bromley North branch and 'Direct' refers to that station specifically.

This rich purple paper denotes that the station is on the route from Charing Cross to Dartford via Greenwich.

Believed to be the earliest type of LCDR luggage label this design, of which there are few survivors, has variations in the layout of the title lines.

The final and commonest LCDR design is well known for being printed on turquoise or blue paper but this destination is unique on this colour background.

This 'standard' LCDR label is mentioned in the main text as being one of very few to non-LCDR destinations..

This is a surprising example of continuity as it was printed in 1946 but harked back to the paper colour used by the LSWR some 50 years earlier despite the fact that almost all labels to the IoW had been printed on white paper since the 1923 grouping..

The Grande Vitesse label mentioned in the main text. The GV depot was situated in Tooley Street close to London Bridge station and these trains from Blackfriars were goods only apparently.

Continuity in the form of an LBSCR style label recreated for the Southern immediately after the grouping and already superseded by the standard SR narrow format white labels.

It would be remiss of the author to ignore the BR/BTC contribution to the world of Southern luggage labels. There were any number of designs all printed on white paper but the printing department topped and tailed the block of sheets with coloured paper which were also distributed.

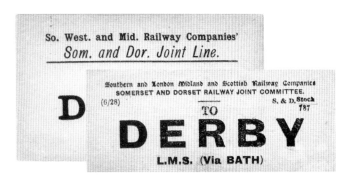

ents or the LSWR mentioning the word 'Halt' whilst there's a solitary mention of "Roffey Road Halt (ex-Fay Gate)" on the LBSCR's labels.

Via, Whence and Green

We all understand the modern term 'cost effective' and one wonders retrospectively about the LBSCR's thought process well into the 20th century. The SR and some of its constituent companies produced luggage labels that were pre-printed with a station of origin but with only a limited number of nominated stations. All the major railways, including the Southern, produced labels from their London main stations, Charing Cross, London Bridge, Cannon Street, Waterloo and Victoria whilst the Lynton & Barnstaple had a small stock from Lynton. There were others dotted around: the LSWR from Southampton West (and in SR days as well), Bournemouth West and Ilfracombe whilst the SER made them from many stations mostly to Cannon Street and Charing Cross. And there are other isolated survivors from the likes of Canterbury West, Margate Sands and Robertsbridge *et al*.

However, The Brighton went completely overboard and all labels were printed with both the station of origin and the destination. Indeed, there are even examples of the earliest type of LBSCR label with the same from-and-to combination but with completely different printings. The Brighton seems to have finally come to its cost-effective senses when it produced 'destination only' labels, to LBSCR stations only and printed on green paper for some reason, early in the last century. Even thereafter it stocked those green labels with origin stations of Victoria, London Bridge, Brighton and Eastbourne. Old habits evidently died hard on that railway as the same practice continued even into early Southern Railway days not only on the green labels but also on white ones as well.

The familiar face of luggage labels is a combination of a company title at the top, a dividing line with the destination occupying much of the remainder of the area. That was certainly true of the early years of labels production but as our railways network increased and travel between railways became more commonplace there came the introduction of a second line underneath the destination and this is generally known as "The via line" although that wasn't always the case as that line sometimes named the destination railway with no indication of how one's luggage was supposed to get to the nominated destination.

There are the inevitable oddities such as the SER labels to Chatham Central that all stated 'SER' underneath the destination but this isn't the place to go into the rivalry and politics that induced the railway to do that. Another reason for a second line became apparent when the Southern was formed as it had to geographically differentiate between identical destination names such as Ashford, Ford and Gillingham that had formerly been in the hands of separate railway companies.

Blankety-blank

Whilst compiling pages for the SEmG web site a few years ago and describing Southern labels the Webmaster asked what railway staff used if there was no label to the required

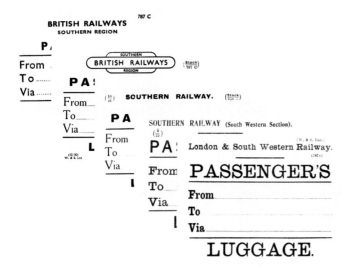

destination held in the station's stock. I was momentarily taken aback as I hadn't described that situation at all! In point of fact the non-availability situation was well catered for on the LBSCR, LSWR, IWR, S&DJC (but only after the grouping) and the Southern with what is generically known as 'the blank label' which is nothing of the sort as there is minimally a company title line. Interestingly, this type of label on the LSWR which, unusually, provided for 'From', 'To' and 'Via' lines is one of the best example of continuity as the identical format continued in production through the SR period and into BR days as shown above.

Transition and continuity

The only significant mergings of railways following the introduction of luggage labels into the railway lexicon were the creation of the SECR in 1899, the 1923 grouping into the Southern Railway and nationalisation in 1948. When the LCDR and SER combined forces luggage label production continued in the tradition of the latter but there are a few notable exceptions which are precisely in the mould of the LCDR's house style but with the title expressed as S. E. & C. & D. Railways. The period immediately following the 1923 grouping is, for many collectors, of great interest as there seems to have been a battle to determine which former

railway's house style should be adopted by the fledgling SR and those labels are described as transitionals. In the event, the LSWR won hands down and subsequent labels produced by the SR, with the notable exception of a few specialised labels, are based on the South Western's house style even down to paper colour in some cases. The clincher is the continued use of the LSWR's stock number '787' for all of its luggage labels which continued even into early BR days.

However, beware the word 'transitional' as it has another, altogether different, meaning in the luggage labels world. There are standard label designs and there are non-standard ones as well such as labels to Europe and the so-called 'Hop-Pickers' labels mentioned later in this article but there's a third category which comprises numbers of different examples that compilers of guides and handbooks are unable to categorise by age and/or design. These invariably attract the descriptive word 'transitionals'.

What's in a date then?

Pre-printed dates on luggage labels can be as significant to a collector as, for instance, the markings on the bases of pottery and can substantially reflect scarcity. A few pre-grouping railways printed production dates (and sometimes print quantities) on their labels with the North Eastern Railway leading the way as far back as 1878. What is interesting to us is that the only SR predecessor to do so was the S&D which undeniably followed its northerly master in that regard and it can be no coincidence that both the Midland and the S&D first adopted the practice in 1900.

The practice of printing production dates became the norm under SR management virtually from the grouping although there are a few examples of plain white SR labels with no date printed on them. There are even a few examples of SECR labels printed in early SR days with a date but no railway title. The S&D continued with the practice, including print quantities, long after the grouping.

For the serious SR labels collector the printing date can be the difference between 'wallpaper' and extreme rarity. There are multiple print dates for most of the SR's stations and also for destinations further afield but it's worth mentioning here the multiplicity of dates on labels with the printed station of origin Waterloo. It transpired from an exchange of e-mails with a former employee in Waterloo station's offices that each department was responsible for its own ordering and stocks of luggage labels with no coordination between those departments hence the range of printing dates on labels for the same destination. It is believed that the accolade for the largest number of known printing dates for a single destination belongs to Portsmouth & Southsea with twenty three. That isn't as strange as it may at first seem as it's an armed forces base of considerable size and other far less likely places such as Bulford have many printing dates for the same reason particularly during and immediately after the Second World War.

To foreign parts we go

The main purpose of luggage labels was to show the destination concisely and the vast majority of those printed were to 'home railway' stations. However, no railway company could live in isolation and so labels were printed to destinations far afield from the points of origin but they were also inclined to be biased towards particular railways mainly because there were through services between the two. One should also bear in mind that the word 'foreign' can be interpreted in another way and that, of course, refers to European destinations.

Arguably the oddest label to another railway in this writer's own SR collection isn't from the Southern at all but emanates from the GER to Central Croydon and is the only reference on a luggage label to that chequered station's life that this author is aware of.

The Southern, obviously as it was part of the system, the LSWR and LBSCR all produced labels to the Isle of Wight but none of the other SR related railways did so. The S&D range of destinations included labels to the SECR, LBSCR and GWR as well its owners the Midland and the LSWR.

The Brighton produced copious amounts from its south coast major stations to LNWR stations as far afield as Bettws-y-Coed and Glasgow whilst those to the GWR included Swansea, Wrexham and Paddington. There are also a couple to the MSWR (*sic*). Further inland there was less evidence of transfer to other railways but East Croydon included many LNWR destinations in its stock whilst there are examples to the SECR, LSWR, LCDR and the IoW plus oddities such as Carshalton to Stalbridge (wrongly credited with LSWR ownership), Thornton Heath to Evercreech and a solitary one from Brighton to Yarmouth on the GER.

The LCDR's 'foreign' contribution amounted to Kentish Tn., King's Cross (GNR) and a non-standard variety, the only example of this style that has come to light, to Harwich via Gravesend Pier which is a classic example of a long-forgotten travel facility.

The LSWR had labels to all the other SR constituent railways and of course had a bond with Derby via the S&D but more on that subject later. Also included in the LSWR mix of labels were destinations on the Bristol & Exeter, the GWR as far west as Penzance, the MSWJR, the Midland up to Carlisle, the NLR and a few to the NER with Newcastle as the most northerly destinations plus copious coverage of the Isle of Wight.

The South Eastern produced an unusual style of label to 'foreign' destinations but again with no company title. They were, printed on a paper colour variously described as buff manilla or even as light as cream and many are adorned with aesthetically pleasing diagonal text within a frame whilst the shapes and sizes of these labels vary considerably. Destinations covered are on the LSWR, LCDR (via STROOD), LBSCR, (via TUN. WELLS), and the GWR (via READING) whilst both the Midland and the LNWR destinations specify the route as being via HERNE HILL.

Surviving luggage labels to European destinations are

quite thin on the ground although the three main constituents of the SR and the Southern itself made provision for such journeys. The LBSCR even went to the trouble of producing Tricoleur coloured labels to Paris whicc was later specified as St. Lazare. The other major change on the LBSCR version of the Tricoleur label is that the former oldest name the "Western Railways of France" in the title lines indicating that the those labels were printed prior to 1908 when that railway became part of the Cdf de l'État which, in its English form of "French State Railway", was incorporated in the title on the later versions of these labels.

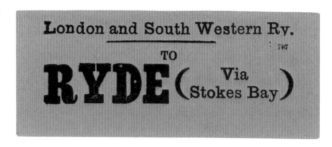

One of the oddities of the labels world is that the SECR, which had steadfastly produced untitled labels, actually did print the company's initials on its labels relating to the continent. By way of an example of how previously unknown material seems to appear from nowhere was the recent (March 2011) acquisition of an SR Grande Vitesse registered luggage labels from Blackfriars to Paris which had never been known of before.

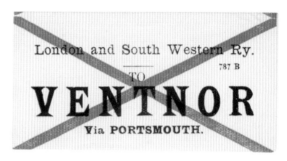

White, Wight and other islands

Mention 'The Island' and the pulse races as well as the price no matter what the genre of collectables. Much of the labels genre relating to the Isle of Wight is unique to the island be that the island's own railways' output or those printed to island destinations. There are LBSCR labels to the likes of Ryde Pier and Cowes that predate the implementation of the island's own railways and the LSWR provided labels on yellow, green or blue paper which suggests that there was some confusion as to which route colour code should be used for the IoW.

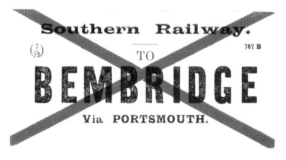

After the arrival of railways on the island two unique characteristics of labels to the island set them apart from their mainland counterparts.

The LSWR produced an incredible number of different labels printed on what's variously described as either mauve or purple paper. Most of those are from Waterloo and what also makes them interesting are the variations of routes printed on the 'Via' lines. Another characteristic of these labels is that they have, generally speaking, not survived the ravages of time very well as they are prone to desiccation and discolouration to almost a biscuit appearance and just as brittle. For all practical purposes those mauve labels were produced to every station on the island.

At an unknown point in time but probably concurrently both the LBSCR and the LSWR supplied luggage labels to the island printed in black on white paper but with a red St. Andrew's cross from corner to corner. Most of the destinations for those labels are on the eastern side of the island but there is an LSWR one to Yarmouth and LBSCR examples to Newport. The LBSCR went a small stage further and produced an oddity in the form of a red cross label with a list of stations under the title line and a blank area under that making, it, one supposes, an IoW 'blank' label.

The SR continued the red cross tradition but for some

reason also produced IoW labels with a blue St. George's cross mainly, again, to stations at the eastern side of the island.

There aren't a vast number of Isle of Wight Railway labels around and even fewer from the Isle of Wight (Newport Junction) Railway. The other railways, even if they did have their own luggage labels, seem to have left us with no survivors. The Southern also printed labels from the IoW to the mainland and these are characterised by "Via Portsmouth" at the bottoms of the labels and some to London termini have that same red/brown St. Andrew's cross or even a brown diamond on them.

Unique amongst the Southern and its constituents are labels to the Channel Islands. There is a non-standard pink label to Jersey which is impossible to apply a date to but the remaining labels, on yellow paper to Guernsey and on blue paper to Jersey, saw design continuity from LSWR days through to the BR era with a constant format and colour as shown below.

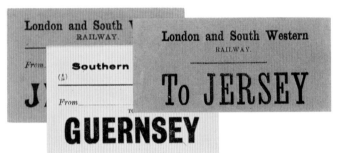

The minor constituents, joint lines, gaffes and oddities

Mention has already been made of the Somerset and Dorset which, as with the Isle of Wight, is widely collected. All destination labels from the S&D were printed in black ink on white paper and there are actually large numbers of survivors but in only limited quantities for any given combination of label type and destination. Those destinations are wide-ranging but to a limited number of other railways in pre-grouping days, GWR, Midland, LSWR, LBSCR, SECR and the S&D itself, whilst after the grouping only the Southern and LMS are represented.

It's perhaps surprising that there are surviving labels from the Lynton and Barnstaple Railway but there are sufficient to provide a flavour of that much lamented railway's labels. They are clearly based on LSWR practice including what have been described as pink labels to LSWR destinations and white for the few others. Despite being a very small concern the railway also had labels with the preprinted station of origin 'Lynton'.

The Plymouth Devonport and South Western Junction's labels have already been mentioned and these are also scarce with only five destinations known and all printed on

white paper but with two designs apparent. Essentially they are the same design at those of the LSWR but wider and thinner in shape

With the notable exception of the S&D joint lines are (almost) never mentioned in SR related label titles despite the fact that they are on tickets. A prime example of this is what is popularly known as the Croydon & Oxted Joint from which there are tickets so titled but the labels emanating there from were issued by the separate companies and there are other such examples in the Portsmouth area as well as Ryde on the Isle of Wight.

The 'almost' above refers to the Sunny South Express labels from Brighton to LNWR destinations but the joint title, Brighton and North Western railways, infers a service as opposed to a jointly operated railway company.

Amongst the most sought after LSWR labels are those that are printed on blue, green or yellow paper with a 'via' line that is routed via the S & D all of which are to Midland Railway destinations. These typically name Evercreech or Templecombe and Bath as the route on the via line..

Special labels were printed by the SECR for use on the famed Hop-Pickers Specials to the hop fields in Kent and that tradition was continued through SR days into the start of the BR era using the same format throughout. The shape and size equate to standard SECR labels and all are printed on coloured paper relative to the group of destinations the pickers were heading for. The paper colours were intended to help with illiteracy amongst the luggage bearers but additionally the first letter of the destination was always printed as a much larger upper case letter than the remainder of the text.

The South Western's labels output also included labels to Jersey and Guernsey. There is one very early example on lilac paper to Jersey but the standard introduced later saw larger format labels on blue paper to Jersey which are prone to fading/dessiccation and on yellow paper to

Guernsey. Both the latter continued with applicable headings through to British Railways days.

The LSWR, IWR, and L&BR all supplied excursion labels printed on red or white paper and these are always a much larger format than the norm for those railways. Gaffes on SR-related labels are few and far between with the best known being West Hoathley as a station of origin on LBSCR labels whilst the LSWR managed to conjure up Itchin Abbas, Meadsted, Freemington, Coppleston, Grately, and Halwell & Beaworthy which, unusually for a typographical error, is amongst the commonest of LSWR labels printed on blue paper. There is allegedly a Brighton label to Cooks Bridge but this writer has never actually seen it and so it might be a myth that's grown over the years. One shouldn't forget, also, "C rystal Pal." emblazoned in red print on an early LBSCR label.

The word "oddities" covers a multitude of sins and one should exercise care as one collector's oddity could be another's commonplace but by way of an example one wonders why LSWR labels to Bentworth & Lasham are available in profusion and yet the other two stations on the Basingstoke and Alton Light Railway, Herriard and Cliddesden, are rarely seen. Much has been made above of the LBSCR's penchant for printing stations of origin but there are many stations from which no examples are known to have survived such as Waddon, Wandsworth Common, Kemp Town and Epsom Downs to name but a few. Quite obscure destination such as California (Belmont), Keymer Junction, Hassocks Gate, York Road (Battersea Park) and Caterham Junction (Purley) are known but Champion Hill and Rotherhithe are missing for example and it seems that no label has come to light for South Bermondsey the latter's successor. Staying with the Brighton, there are labels to Selsey which was presumably on Col. Stephens' Hundred of Manhood and Selsey Tramway and also to East Selsey which, for this writer, is something of a mystery but perhaps the Southern Way's readership has the answer to that conundrum.

The mundane

The preceding text has covered a large amount of data, applicable illustrations and some historical background information and mention has been made of "standard" and "the familiar face of" our railway luggage labels but for the most part those haven't been illustrated. There was, as ever, a good reason for that as the author's brief was to optimise the colour aspect but on reading the first draft of this article Hon. Ed. Strongly hinted that an extra page could be accommodated.and so where better to illustrate the ordinary?

The LSWR era of labels associated with routes by colour lasted approximately from the 1850's until the 1880's by which time it seems that there was a general shift to the use of blue paper regardless of route. There was then a shift to white labels with the exception of the IoW. There were

two basic printing styles for those white labels as shown below with the 'From' line being a quite short lived variety.

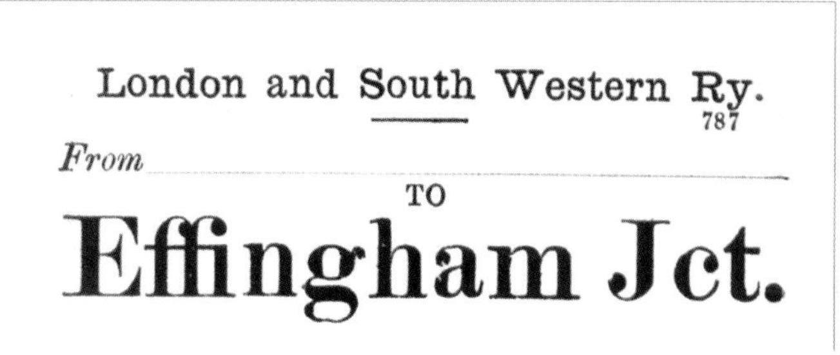

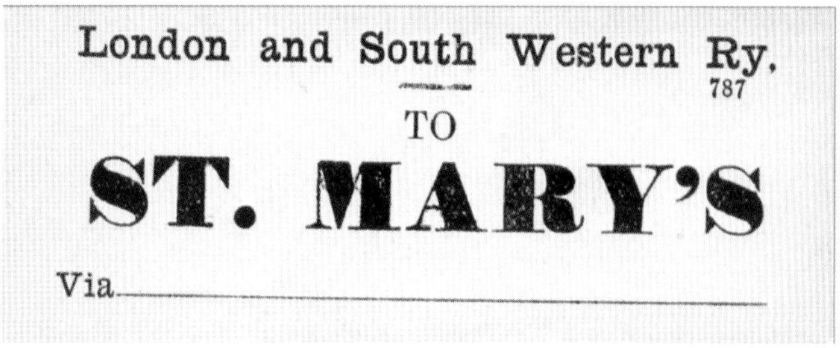

The LBSCR's earliest labels are illustrated elsewhere in this article and were followed by the style described as transitional. The example shown here, a scarce one from Norbury, also typifies the problems caused by desiccation and poor storage.

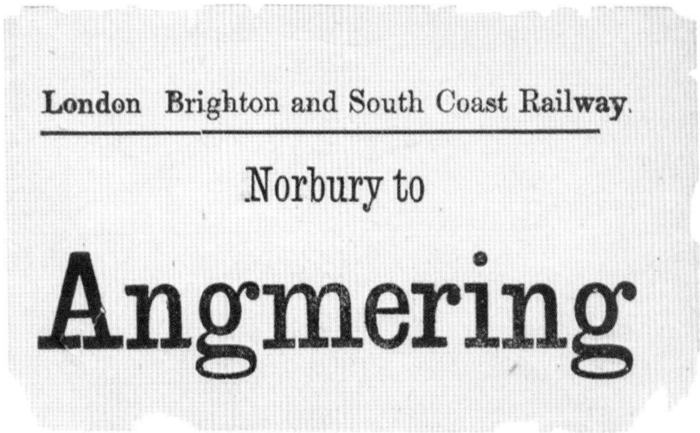

The most commonly known style of LBSCR label was also printed black on white paper and there tens of thousands of them out there making them remarkable survivors in this world of disposable commodities. The example shown, from

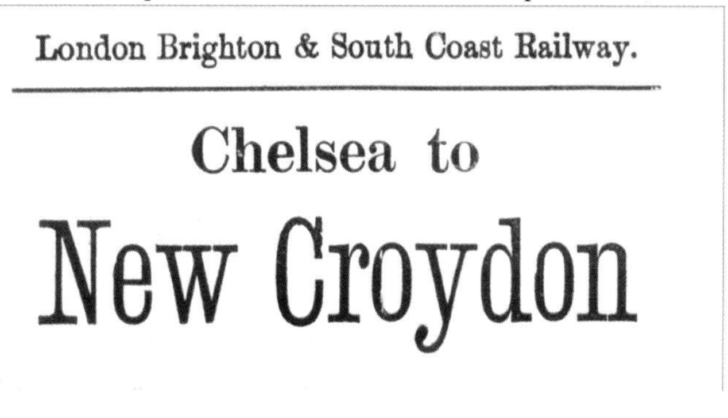

Chelsea to New Croydon, is a very common one and exemplifies again that relatively short-lived station names are the more likely ones to have survived.

...... and those colour coded labels ......

The SER, SECR, IWR and LSWR all made use of coloured labels by route but the SE(C)R, which continued the policy right through The Grouping, is far too complex to explain here and so only the LSWR's policy is listed here and even this is necessarily only summarised.

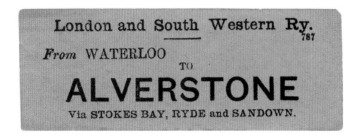

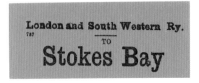

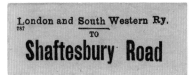

WHITE: former London & Southampton Railway stations.

YELLOW: Bournemouth to Weymouth except the Swanage branch; GWR; MSWJR; Metropolitan; NLR; S&D; MR via the S&D; a few to the IoW.

GREY: Overton Grately (sic); Whitchurch and Porton but only until +/- 1861.

ORANGE: LBSCR coastal stations and a couple just inland. One oddity to Addlestone.

GREEN: Portsmouth area. Midland via the S & D.

PINK: stations north of the London & Southampton main line. Guildford to Havant. WLER through to Richmond.

BLUE: all stations west of Oakley plus a few GWR west of Exeter. There was a shift to blue when route coding ended in the 1880's.

PURPLE: Isle of Wight destinations which include both Totland Bay and Alum Bay.

Routes yet again but for the last time

Several times in the preceding text there have been statements about routes but there is a type of label which is actually known as a routing label as shown here.

These labels differ from the normal label types because the destinations are railways as opposed to a station although some do leave a space for a destination to be written in and they are nearly always considerably larger than the standard issues. Most originate with the LSWR plus a

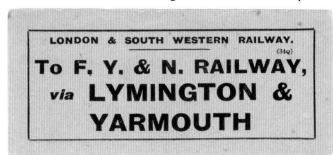

few from the PDSWJR, the LCDR and The Brighton. What piques the inetrest in the example shown is the stock number '34G' which one would normally associate with the LBSCR all of whose 'red cross' labels bear a '34' code

---

One hopes that the variety of luggage labels produced in the south of England for more than a century has captured the reader's attention and that said reader has been encouraged to root out those labels that were accumulated a half century ago and to take a longer look at them in the light of what has been written here.

Sources: illustrations from the author's collection and that of Godfrey Croughton. plus essential support from Brian J. Harding who proofread the first draft. My grateful thanks are extended to both those gentlemen. Reference was also made to the Railway Print Society guides to luggage labels.

There must be some luggage labels somewhere….!

The classic Brighton Line location. Marsh '13' tank No. 22 of 1908 on the Quarry line.

ASHFORD TO BRIGHTON (via Stoke)

Basil K. Field - Locomotive Engineer

Philip Atkins

The kaleidoscopic diversity of the pre-1923 British locomotive scene can be ascribed to a relatively small number of largely unknown yet highly skilled locomotive draughtsmen who, in the furtherance of their modestly paid careers, frequently migrated between the drawing offices of both the main line railways, and sometimes also those of the parallel commercial British locomotive building industry. As a direct result, notwithstanding the many distinctive individual house styles of the different railway companies, it was possible for a keen observer sometimes to discern unmistakeably similar characteristic features on the locomotives of two (or more) disparate railways. For example, such affinities could be detected between the locomotives of the South Eastern & Chatham, North Staffordshire and London, Brighton & South Coast railways after 1900, but who or what was the link?

Basil Kingsford Field was born in Lee in Kent in 1866, the fifth of a large family of six children, of whom both an elder brother and sister had been born in Chile. Despite seemingly humble origins Field proceeded to enjoy a remarkably erudite education for that period, ie initially at Dulwich College, in Heidelberg, King's College (London), Crystal Palace School of Engineering, and finally the London Technical Institute. Having completed his formal education he then served his time at the Ashford Works of the South Eastern Railway, presumably as a premium apprentice of James Stirling. His first entry in the (copy) Ashford drawing register, now in the National Railway Museum archives, is dated 8 August 1893. He was promoted to chief draughtsman remarkably soon afterwards, either in 1895 or 1897 according to source, but following the institution of the working alliance of the SER with the smaller London Chatham & Dover Railway in 1899, the latter's chief draughtsman from Longhedge Works (Battersea) moved to take charge at Ashford. A Geordie by birth, and ex-Robert Stephenson & Co. in Newcastle, Robert Surtees was some eleven years older than Basil Field. A photograph of the small Ashford drawing office staff in June 1900 shows Surtees and Field sitting side by side, constituting the front row, but whereas the neatly moustached Surtees looks confi-

Right - Ashford Drawing Office, circa 1900. Back row unknown. Front row: left - Basil K Field. Centre - James Clayton. Right - A J Tassell.

dently and squarely at the camera, Field, a darkly handsome man with a prominent 'Wyatt Earp' moustache, by contrast appears distinctly ill at ease. By all accounts Surtees was fiercely pro-LC&D, and one wonders what tensions existed between the two 'factions' which had now doubtless unwillingly been brought together at Ashford. Surtees was the true architect of the celebrated Wainwright Class D 4-4-0, whose elegant lines were further enhanced by the elaborate new SE& CR rich green livery. Oddly enough, in *style* this had actually been directly derived from the former LC&D *black* locomotive livery, a variant of which was also employed on the Hull & Barnsley Railway throughout its existence, stemming from the fact that Thomas Kirtley had overseen the provision of its early locomotives, the first 0-6-0s having been virtual copies of his engines on the LC&DR.

In another photograph of similar date, from which Surtees is absent, Field this time appears distinctly more upbeat. Present in both photographs is a young James Clayton, who had arrived from Beyer, Peacock & Co. in 1899, whose first task at Ashford had been to design the frames for the new Class C 0-6-0, going on to design the cab and splashers for the Class D 4-4-0, and in October 1900 even sketching out a proposed inside cylinder 0-8-0. Also in both photographs is A J Tassell, who left Ashford in 1901 for a

short spell in the design office of Neilson Reid & Co. in Glasgow (then the largest British locomotive builder) before joining the North Staffordshire Railway at Stoke as its chief draughtsman in 1902.

Field's final entry in the Ashford drawing register was dated 24 April 1902, and Clayton similarly signed off just three weeks later. On 17 June 1902 the Traffic & Finance Committee of the North Staffordshire Railway minuted '*Appointment of Works Manager. Mr Basil Field of the South Eastern Railway was appointed at a salary of £5 per week from the 1st July 1902.*'

However, only barely four months later, on 7 October 1902, the same committee recorded '*Works Manager Locomotive Dept. Mr John Albert Hookham was appointed in place of Mr Field resigned, and on the same terms, viz: £5 per week for the term of 3 years.*'

Two months later still, on 2 December 1902, the minutes recorded '*Mr B Field late Locomotive Works Manager. Work to be provided for him till the end of the year.*' The circumstances underlying Field's resignation yet initially continuing employment at Stoke remain a mystery.

Basil Field's chief at Stoke was John H Adams (son of William Adams), the locomotive, carriage and wagon superintendent, who had only been appointed himself the previous March, after having been assistant works manager at Ashford, and so the two men would have been well acquainted. John Hookham, a former Longhedge man, had moved to Ashford drawing office with Surtees, and had become actively involved in the design of the Wainwright D class 4-4-0 boiler before moving to Brazil in 1900 to become locomotive superintendent of the Donna Thereza Christina Railway, a post which had previously been held by Adams between 1887 and 1898.

On taking office Adams swiftly ordered six 0-6-2 tank engines for the North Staffs from the Vulcan Foundry,

which were duly delivered in 1903, whose chimneys were pure SER in outline. In other respects the engines also almost amounted to tank versions of the Wainwright Class C 0-6-0, and during this period Harry Wainwright on the South Eastern & Chatham, as it was now styled, himself contemplated building some 0-6-2Ts, which in the event did not progress beyond the drawing board. The NSR engines were described in *The Railway Magazine* for January 1904, where it was stated '*reversing is effected by steam on the ordinary steam and cataract cylinder principle, but worked on a new system by means of Field's patent valves, which, from the cab, actuate the steam cylinder piston, and automatically act so that the moving to any position of a small lever in a notch plate, is followed by the movement of the weigh shaft lever to the corresponding point desired.*' British patent (13365/1903) had been granted to Field in June 1903. These engines set the general style, including chimney-wise, for all subsequent NSR locomotives built (at Stoke by the Company itself), including the now preserved 0-6-2T No.2, over the next twenty years.

By this time, however, having married Alice Caroline Brown in Wandsworth in the spring of 1903, Field was working in Coventry as the works manager of the Motor Manufacturing Company, on which James Clayton was also employed as a draughtsman and later assistant works manager. (Clayton had presumably arrived in Coventry first but in late 1904 was *privately* recruited by Cecil Paget on the Midland Railway to design his revolutionary and rarely seen *eight* cylinder 2-6-2 locomotive No.2299, before he later joined the regular MR design staff. He would return to Ashford as chief draughtsman in early 1914). In this new branch of technology Field was granted a further patent (14488/1906) which related to motor vehicle suspension, but by the time this in turn was published in June 1907 he was back in railway service once again, this time on the London,

Former LBSCR 'E2' type 0-6-0 with original side tanks. The engine may be No. 100, and has been modified from the original with the addition of vacuum brakes. The location is not reported but may be New Cross in Southern Railway days.

Locomotive testing from Brighton, 30 June 1907. Basil K. Field has the bowler-hat on the left, on the right is Herbert Buckle from the drawing office.

Brighton & South Coast Railway as chief draughtsman at Brighton. (Field was by now the father of a young daughter born in Coventry. His move to the LBSCR proved to be prudent as the Motor Manufacturing Company, which had started out in Coventry in 1897, removed to Clapham in south London in 1907 and failed the following year).

On many railways chief draughtsmen were above actually producing drawings, but Basil Field's first entries in the Brighton drawing register (original now at York) appeared in February 1907. He swiftly designed a replacement standard cast iron chimney for the Stroudley standard locomotive classes which in profile was pure Stirling SER but enhanced by a slight cap. Other versions were soon adopted on new construction and also retro-fitted to Robert Billinton locomotives (including the now preserved 0-6-2T No.473 *Birch Grove*). A much shorter variant, only 18 inches tall, was fitted to the Lawson Billinton 4-6-4 express tanks (of 1914-22) to be mentioned later, which interestingly was closely mirrored by the 20 inch casting on the North Staffordshire Railway New F 0-6-4Ts (built 1916-19), designed under A J Tassell prior to his promotion to works manager at Stoke in 1915, in succession to Hookham following John Adams' death. Ironically, the original Stirling SER chimney which had been the ancestor of both would have almost certainly become extinct in Kent by this time.

Field's chief at Brighton was the evidently extremely disagreeable Douglas Earle Marsh, but he enthusiastically supported the decision which Marsh had evidently already made to experiment with locomotive superheating,

which previously had only been tried on the Great Western Railway, on a 'Saint' 4-6-0, and by the Lancashire & Yorkshire Railway on a pair of 0-6-0s in 1906. Under Field's direction drawings for the piston valve cylinders and superheated boiler for an express inside cylinder 4-4-2T were prepared in mid-1907. No.22 was completed at Brighton in March 1908 and its dramatic reduction in fuel and water consumption really put superheating on the map as far as British locomotive practice was concerned, such that it was being very widely adopted in new construction by 1912. This engine should have been an eminent candidate for official preservation upon its eventual withdrawal by British Railways in 1951. Interestingly, their Belpaire fireboxes apart, some remarkably similar superheated express passenger 4-4-2Ts were built by the North Staffordshire Railway at Stoke in 1911, which enjoyed very much shorter working lives which terminated in the early 1930s under LMS auspices.

Field's job also included locomotive testing. He appears in a photograph, bowler-hatted, standing in the indicator shelter fitted to Marsh 4-4-2 No.39 awaiting departure from Brighton Station, while at the other side (wearing a flat cap) stood Herbert Buckle, a Brighton draughtsman, who many years later would write Field's obituary. The date would have been 30 June 1907, when on the down run No.39 developed a very respectable peak IHP (indicated horsepower) of 1402 at a speed of 53mph and 50 per cent cut-off when passing Stoat's Nest (now Coulsdon North).

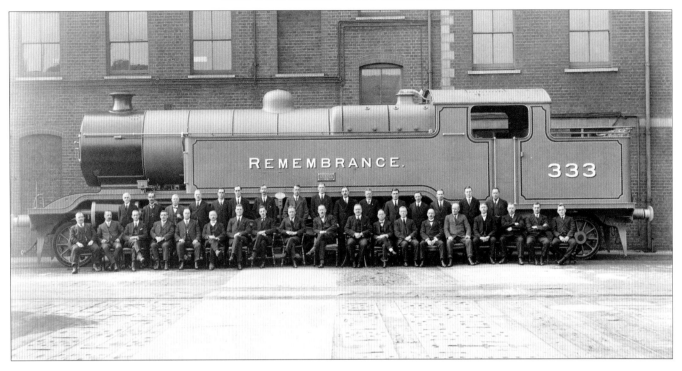

Officers group at Brighton alongside 'L' class 4-6-4T No. 333 'Remembrance'. This was the last locomotive built by the LBSCR and was named in honour of Brighton employees killed in WW1.

Back on the design front Field would have been very closely involved with the design of the Class J express passenger outside cylinder 4-6-2T, of which the first of only two was completed at Brighton in December 1910, which made it the first new British locomotive design to be designed from scratch to incorporate a superheater. These were later developed under Marsh's successor into the imposing Class L 4-6-4T as Marsh resigned, or was requested to resign, allegedly on health grounds, in late 1911. In September 1911 Field produced a diagram for a 'Proposed Goods Tank Engine'. This showed an 8ft + 8ft coupled wheelbase and was to become the extremely neat Class E2 0-6-0T, first built in 1913, although a subsequent diagram for this made a few weeks later had the total wheelbase reduced to 15ft 3in. (which was not adopted). Field's final entry as a draughtsman, which related to steam heating, was made on 30 December 1911.

Robert Billinton's son, Lawson, was appointed to succeed Marsh, and he promoted Field to works manager, effective from 1 January 1912, at a salary of £480. New construction during 1912 was largely confined to the final batch of superheated Class I3 4-4-2Ts and the second 4-6-2T, but 1913 witnessed the construction of the first Class K 2-6-0s and E2 0-6-0Ts. April 1914 saw the emergence of the first Brighton 4-6-4T, which had first been outlined in diagram form in December 1912 (just as Beyer, Peacock & Co. were delivering the first British 'Baltic' tanks, which had originally been ordered by the London, Tilbury &

Southend Railway, to the Midland Railway which had very recently absorbed that company in the meantime). There are strong indications that it was originally intended to build the second engine instead as a 4-6-0, for which an additional K class tender was apparently built, although there is no indication of such a proposal in the Brighton drawing register. The outbreak of the First World War severely curtailed new construction at Brighton, although five additional 2-6-0s were turned out during 1916 with government approval. Basil Field, again with bowler hat, was photographed standing by an almost complete but unpainted No. 346. An immediate post-war proposal to build a 2-6-2T version was not acceptable to the civil engineer (although somewhat surprisingly its *estimated* maximum axleload remained precisely the same at 19.75 tons), and ten more 2-6-0s were ordered instead, of which only seven were in the event built. For these ten boiler shells were unusually fabricated by the Midland Railway at Derby, such was the heavy backlog of locomotive repair work then confronting Brighton Works and Basil Field, who as works manager was further challenged by a series of industrial disputes.

A proposal to build eight more 'Baltic' tanks was also curtailed to only five, the last of which, No.333, was completed in April 1922 and named *Remembrance* a year later. (It is curious that although delivery of the 2-6-0s commenced in September 1913, two months before the first 4-6-4Ts were authorised, their numbering had commenced at

ASHFORD to BRIGHTON (via Stoke)

337. This would have allowed for the three further 4-6-4Ts had they been built nine years later).

On his discharge from the Army the late Alastair (A B) Macleod entered Brighton Works as one of five new apprentices in May 1919, which brought him into weekly contact with Basil Field whom he fondly recalled (when aged eighty eight) to the writer in 1988: *"I remember he gave us all a dressing down for wasting too much time having morning coffee at 'Fred's snack hut' on the main arrival platform at Brighton Central Station; he threatened to make it out of bounds.....I always felt he had good reason to tick one off for a misdemeanour.........Towards the end of my time at Brighton Works (in 1922) I grew to like him very much, as we had a mutual interest in model and miniature railways. Field had a great friend named Leigh Pemberton who owned a large estate at Torry Hill in Kent. Together they made an extensive 9 inch gauge railway in the grounds. Field told me all about this, and gave me a blue print of the general arrangement of an engine he built for the line. A model of an NER Worsdell 'I' class 4-2-2."* (This was

Basil K. Field - Locomotive Engineer

named *Robin* after John Leigh Pemberton's young son, who would later become the Governor of the Bank of England, and who is now Lord Kingsdown.)

Although not yet sixty, Basil Field retired in 1924 and devoted the rest of his life to model locomotive building. A former next door neighbour recalled him building a 15 inch gauge model steam locomotive in his terraced house at 16 Chatsworth Road in central Brighton, close to the Works, and hearing its whistle blow in the back garden signifying its completion. He also remembered Field for his liking for an early morning dip in the sea nearby, and for his lively sense of humour and penning of humorous ditties. His sense of humour and wide circle of friends was also recalled in his obituary in *The Locomotive Magazine* for December 1941, following his death in Brighton on 15 November. Tragically, Alice, his wife of nearly forty years, also died just five days later, unlike that of her husband her death received a mention in *The Times*.

The writer is indebted for the assistance of Mike Fell in the preparation of this article.

Brand new 'K' class 2-6-0, destined to become No. 346 at Brighton in 1916. Basil K. Field is the first man in from the left.

THE SOUTHERN TRAVELLER'S HANDBOOK 1965/66

Jeffery Grayer in recalling a little remembered publicity exercise, the first Southern Region Handbook of 45 years ago, reminisces over some long lost railway facilities and reviews the Handbook's contents with the benefit of that wonderful thing - hindsight!

Going to press for the first time in June 1965 the innovative "**Southern Traveller's Handbook**" set out, as the Introduction by David McKenna the Southern Region's General Manager specified, to *"interest customers and provide useful information on the services of BR in general and of the SR in particular."* Running to 320 pages its production costs were largely covered by advertising and revenue from sales, retailing at 7/6d (37.5p), thereby scotching in advance any adverse publicity regarding spending fare payers' money on public relations exercises. The opportunity was taken to explain some of the region's problems and to publicise their achievements but the prime purpose was to produce *"a book of value to all who live in the South."*

As the front cover indicated, it was directed to a number of specific customer groups who warranted a section devoted to their needs, many sections being written by journalists or well known writers and broadcasters. In addition to the 10 mentioned on the cover Househunters, Campers, Coast-goers and Freighters were catered for although the "Tourists" mentioned on the cover did not feature inside by name presumably being covered by other chapters. An explanatory map showing the three divisions of the SR followed the Introduction with the Divisional Managers being identified together with the Chief Shipping and Continental Manager. A glance at the map, accompanying photographs of the Divisional Managers, revealed the 1963 boundary changes which had controversially awarded chunks of the former SR to the WR, the boundaries now being at Wilton South, Dorchester West, Dilton Marsh and Blandford Forum. A number of lines shown as open in 1965 were subsequently to close, the Beeching proposals still being worked through at that time. These lines were –

Reading Southern	1965
S&D	1966
Cowes – Ryde	1966
Shanklin – Ventnor	1966
Shoreham – Horsham	1966
Three Bridges – Tunbridge Wells	1967
Appledore – New Romney	1967
Hailsham – Polegate	1968
Romsey – Eastleigh	1969
(subsequent re-opening to passengers in 2003)	
Lewes – Uckfield	1969

Wareham – Swanage	1972	preservation line
Winchester – Alton	1973	preservation line
Eridge – Tunbridge Wells	1985	preservation line

Poignantly the map shows an arrow from Salisbury pointing west to "Exeter, Plymouth, Padstow, Bude and Ilfracombe", all to succumb to the rundown under WR control and subsequent closure with the exception of the largely singled route to Exeter.

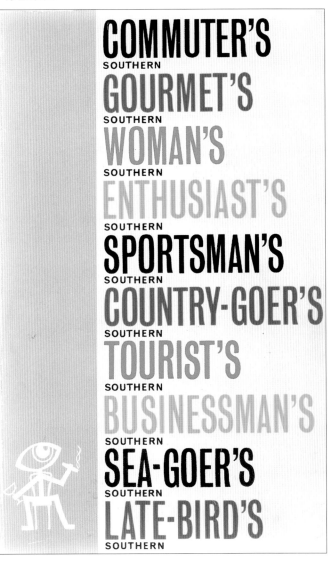

COMMUTER'S
SOUTHERN
GOURMET'S
SOUTHERN
WOMAN'S
SOUTHERN
ENTHUSIAST'S
SOUTHERN
SPORTSMAN'S
SOUTHERN
COUNTRY-GOER'S
SOUTHERN
TOURIST'S
SOUTHERN
BUSINESSMAN'S
SOUTHERN
SEA-GOER'S
SOUTHERN
LATE-BIRD'S
SOUTHERN

The first section kicks off with perhaps the life-blood of the SR – **Commuters**. *"Commuting is disagreeable. Wasteful of time, money, energy – but also, it seems, an inevitable consequence of material prosperity."* This is the opening contention which is as true today as it was back in 1965. Great emphasis was placed on *"commuting in reverse"*, several cases of high profile firms such as Brown & Polson, Dorothy Perkins, Unilever subsidiaries and Sun Alliance moving out of London being cited as being assisted by the work of the Location of Offices Bureau. As the advertising said "The time to leave the Jungle is NOW !"

Issued in the interests of better business and living by The Location of Offices Bureau
Telephone HOL 2921

The second section addresses the **Businessman** with its list of principal business trains from London to all parts of the country. A map purporting to show the rail routes linking the main centres of population and industry contains some latter day casualties such as the Waverley route, The Great Central, the ex LSWR Exeter – Plymouth route and the East Lincolnshire line. Facilities include the Business Season ticket whereby companies with a freight bill in excess of £2,500 pa are able to have such a season ticket for a nominated representative at 25% below the ordinary rate.

The **Woman's** Southern section naturally focuses on shopping in London, of course, but also mentioned are Bournemouth, Brighton, Canterbury, Guildford, Southampton and Tunbridge Wells. Bournemouth in those days still boasted a number of large department stores, many of which are no longer with us – Beales, Bealesons, Bobbys, Plummer Roddis (Closed 1973), Williams and Hopkins, Brights and J J Allens. Some of the ideas such as holding a fashion show on board the train may seem a little farfetched now and the *"Go Ma'm Go"* slogan used to advertise women's' party bookings, such as the 669 women from Kent who went to London for a day out, taking in the "Sound of Music" at the Palace Theatre, are definitely dated. They used separate trains starting from Margate and Sandwich the units joining at Ashford, the all-in fare costing 27/-. Shepherding the on-board throng were two BR couriers, male numbers being boosted by two or three husbands who also made the trip – *"I've no fears"*, said one of them, *"I tell myself I'm in charge of them. This is a jolly good day out and the girls are great fun."*

YOU CAN EVEN HOLD A FASHION SHOW ON A TRAIN

The **Househunter's** Southern is particularly revealing with some of the house prices mentioned being unbelievable in today's climate. Enhancements in local prices resulting from electrification of local railway lines is of course stressed and great hopes for increased prices were held out for the forthcoming Bournemouth electrification – *"If you are toying with the idea of making a move it might be worth taking a look at what is available in Hampshire – before the prices there go chasing those of Sussex and Surrey."* The Harestock estate near Winchester for example had houses ranging from £3,500 to £6,500. Alresford, which unfortunately was to lose its rail connection in 1973, had 3 bedroom semis for just £4,000.

The **Sportsman's** Southern held out the prospect of county cricket at a number of grounds in Kent, Sussex, Surrey and Hampshire, and tennis at Wimbledon of course, but mention was made of other major tennis venues at Beckenham, Guildford, Bournemouth, Ryde, Winchester and Bognor Regis. When the move to a site between Wimbledon and Southfields was made in 1922 to accommodate the larger facilities required, some lines of Kipling were apparently engraved above the Centre Court which could be usefully recalled in today's aggressive, financially motivated world of tennis – *"If you can meet with triumph and disaster, and treat these two Imposters just the same."*

Football was played by major teams in the south although today some of the grounds have changed - the Goldstone ground of Brighton & Hove Albion is now a retail park, The Dell is no longer Southampton's ground being a housing estate, Millwall now play at the New Den not The Den and Reading at Madjeski Stadium rather than Elm Park. Horse racing continues today at all the courses named with the exception of Wye which held its last meeting in May 1974. Rugby and golf complete the line-up of sports catered for by SR services.

The **Gourmet's** Southern article was written by the well-known broadcaster Wynford Vaughan-Thomas who opined that the SR lines carried *"travellers through the heart of gastronomic England. Even 10 years ago I would not have dared to write an article about food in the Southern Region. What few gastronomic standards our island once had became casualties in World War Two. A conscientious eater as he surveyed the scene in 1945, would have seen nothing but the wreckage of snoek* (a wartime fish staple from South Africa), *soya links and sauce bottles strewn over the embattled tables of Britain."* He goes on to mention several eating establishments in London remarking that in Lyons Steak Houses, for example, you get an excellent steak for about 8/6d !

Tourist's Southern is a largely pictorial section detailing the delights of Stonehenge, the White Cliffs of Dover, Brighton Pavilion, the Needles Isle of Wight and Beaulieu Abbey and Museum amongst others. This is followed by **Camper's** Southern, the camper in Southern territory being particularly fortunate in that many of the campsites in the four counties are *"within easy reach of a railway station and nearly all are on bus routes which connect with rail services."* Whilst increasing emphasis has been placed on better rail/bus connections in recent years with bus and rail companies often under the same privatised banner, I'm not sure that being *"within easy reach of a railway station"* still holds true with the line closures of the intervening 45 years.

Dancing their way across Europe – all night long!

One of the attractions of continental rail travel extolled in this section is the "Snowsports Special" leaving from Victoria station at 09.30 on Sunday mornings, the continental portion of which from/to Calais carries the "Snowsports Inn". This is a specially converted carriage, devoid of all internal partitions, fitted with a dance floor and equipped at one end with a well-stocked bar.

One aspect of camping which has certainly ceased is the Camping Coach where six people could be accommodated for between £6- £17 per week, locations on the SR being at Amberley, Birchington-on-Sea, Corfe Castle, Hinton Admiral, Lyndhurst Road, Martin Mill, Sandling, Sway, Walmer, Wool and Yalding. The number of camping coaches offered for hire declined from the mid-1960s as other forms of holidays became more popular, the condition of the vehicles deteriorated, and the number of staffed stations at which they could be sited decreased with line closures. The last were offered to the public by the London Midland Region in 1971, although some were retained for many years after this for railway staff to hire for their holidays at Dawlish Warren and Marazion. Holiday camps also featured in this section there being some 30 on the SR at this time from the small Woodlands near Sevenoaks, accommodating 110 people to Butlins at Bognor Regis catering for 8,000. Gibson's Camp at Bracklesham Bay offered a more

Right - *RCD 577 my father's green Morris Minor being loaded onto the plane at Lydd.*

The **Countrygoer's** Southern focused on walking in the countryside, a task made much more pleasant by the ease with which the countryside could be reached – by SR train of course ! In tackling the Pilgrim's Way from Canterbury to Winchester for example, a journey that would have taken Chaucer's Pilgrims several weeks , there would have been no easy way of returning home in the interim in Chaucer's day but our author was able to accomplish this trek in sections in 10 days and could spend every night at home in

intimate type of holiday apparently with accommodation for 400 and featuring a special "den" for teenagers complete with "*beat group*".

London as well courtesy of the train which returned him home at night and brought him out in the morning to a number of convenient break points along the route. The SR's famous "Ramblers Specials" took thousands of walkers out into the countryside on Sundays from Easter until the middle of September. *"Don't be put off by the idea of an organised ramble. There's nothing regimented about any of them, they're more of a gentle stroll with an experienced guide to help you see everything that's worth seeing."*

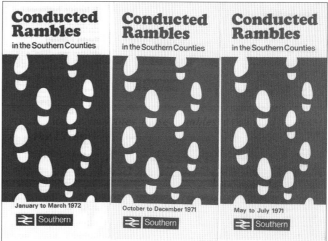

As the above indicates these rambles continued at least into the 1970s.

The SR were not averse to advertising alternative ways of reaching the continent and I can vividly recall travelling with my father's Morris Minor aboard a Silver City Bristol freighter in 1959 en route to Italy via the link from Lydd (Ferryfield) to Le Touquet, Silver City becoming part of British United Airways in 1962.

The **Coastgoer's** Southern begins with a potted history of the development of one of the first railway lines from London to the south coast, that to Brighton in 1841 with extensive quotes from "The Times" of the period.

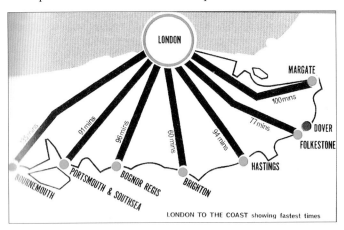

LONDON TO THE COAST showing fastest times

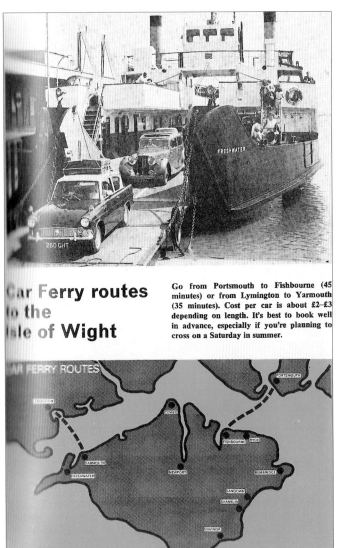

Car Ferry routes to the Isle of Wight

Go from Portsmouth to Fishbourne (45 minutes) or from Lymington to Yarmouth (35 minutes). Cost per car is about £2–£3 depending on length. It's best to book well in advance, especially if you're planning to cross on a Saturday in summer.

A comparison of fastest times 45 years ago, seen above, and in 2010 reveals that following the Bournemouth electrification of 1967 the greatest improvement in fastest journey times to those shown above is that to Bournemouth which has been reduced to 103minutes from 135 minutes, the others such as Portsmouth, with only a 3 minute improvement to 88 minutes, and Brighton with a 9 minute improvement are more marginal.

The **Sea-Goer's** Southern deals with services using car and ship and train and ship, principally the "Golden Arrow" and the "Night Ferry", the former ceasing to run in September 1972 with the latter finishing in October 1980. Channel Islands services via Weymouth Quay are mentioned as are the relatively new ships Caesarea and Sarnia built in 1960 which controversially for the time were one class only which brought **"no little criticism at the outset"** in those class conscious days. Regular passenger services to the Quay at Weymouth finished in 1987. It was suggested that passengers to the Channel Islands could hire a car or scooter whilst there as *"petrol costs about 3/- a gallon".* Cross Channel car ferry routes are covered next as are crossings to the Isle of Wight, European car sleeper routes and not forgetting BR's own car carrying services, although of course the SR's pioneering Surbiton – Okehampton route had been quietly dropped the previous year in 1964 through declining patronage. Inserted into this section is some advice about the new continental level crossing barriers coming into use at this time.

The section entitled **Enthusiast's** Southern, written by Ian Allan himself, recognised the interest of the railway enthusiast and began with a potted history of the SR since 1923. Locomotive development was summarised concluding with the statement that *"today there is very little steam left on the region – and this will be completely eliminated when the Bournemouth line goes over to electric traction."* This duly occurred in July 1967 although a little later than planned. Despite all the modernity of the railway there was still *"plenty of steam trains on the lines to Bournemouth and the south west whilst the well maintained pre-SR rolling stock hauled by cheerful equally veteran tank engines with their distinctive deep throated hooters are part of the fascination for young holidaymakers to the Isle of Wight".* I'm not sure this description of the 02s, which were just about on their last legs by the end, really holds true. Steam finished on the island at the end of 1966 which also saw closure of the lines from Shanklin to Ventnor and Ryde to Cowes. Ian Allan pointed out that Clapham Museum hosted several items of SR rolling stock, which subsequently moved to York in 1975 upon closure of Clapham. Half a dozen further locomotives were also noted as stored on the Eastern Region, at Stratford, pending restoration and of course the Bluebell Railway, one of the few preservation sites at that time, comes in for a mention as the place to see SR locomotives in action. Few could have foreseen at that

Some of the delights awaiting the Southern Latebird at London clubs in the Swinging Sixties.

time the burgeoning preservation scene that was to follow in later years.

The **Freighter's** Southern opens with the nightly take-over of the tracks by freight trains now that the commuters are home and in bed. The age of freight trains as *"slow-moving clanking, banging and grinding monstrosities"* was changing fast with new look overnight services from the South Coast to the Midlands and the North. Such services as the "Solent" freighter from Southampton, the "Midland-Merseyman" from Brighton and "Medway-Lancastrian" were much vaunted as the new face of freight handling. Block trains with their mammoth loads such as oil from Fawley, cement from Cliffe in Kent, and roadstone from Wrexham for the Sevenoaks by-pass were apparently the shape of things to come. Bananas from Southampton Docks, now a thing of the past as far as rail is concerned, warranted 400 special trains in the mid-1960s. Even the humble sugar beet gets a mention in the shape of the rail-head developed at Lavant on the former Chichester – Midhurst line, taking the crop 160 miles by rail to Kidderminster for refining. The last sugar beet run on this line was in January 1970.

The final section is the **Latebird's** Southern dealing with night life in the capital and showing the first trains home in the early hours to a variety of destinations. *"Why rush home – Go home with the milk and the newspapers"* says the commentator - commodities now alas also lost to rail. Clubs a - plenty are detailed such as the Astor Club in Berkeley Square, where there was no entrance fee but the minimum charge for dinner was one guinea (whatever happened to those !) whilst a double scotch and soda would set you back 11/-. Those were the days !

Each station on the SR was mentioned in the final **Gazetteer** section at the end of the book with opening times of booking offices shown such as that for Blandford Forum, with the quaintly-sounding telephone number Blandford 2941, which, surprisingly less than a year before closure in March 1966, was open until 22.00 at night, together with fares and journey times to London.

BLANDFORD FORUM
   P T EC-Weds MD-Thurs
Telephone   Blandford 2941

Ticket Office Open
            Weekdays only 07 30–22 00

Fares to London
            1st Cl. Single 52s 6d
            2nd Cl. Single 35s 0d
            Off Peak Return 36s 0d
            Quarterly Season £56 1s 0d
Fastest journey time to London 196 mins.

Whilst we should not be surprised at the inflationary increases since 1965/66 I suppose what really strikes home is the sense of how rapidly many facets of the railway, which the writers of the time obviously thought were here to stay, withered and died away so quickly such that the railway of 2012 is almost unrecognisable from that of 47 years ago.

ANOTHER BULLEID ENIGMA?

Thought there was nothing more to say about Mr Bulleid and his time on the Southern, well read on! Paul Russenberger has come up with an interesting comment on how his influence may have been far more widespread than first thought and which is explained by the Editor.

In a recent Editorial in 'SW' I raised the question about how much more there really is to unearth about some of the well-known players in railway history. Certain individuals, notably Robert Urie, are an obvious exception but considering the likes of Mr Bulleid and his products and in particular his influence, it is probably unlikely there is much new to be uncovered. Or is there?

I first met Paul Russenberger at an exhibition in 2009. He kindly introduced himself (I was very pleased he did) and we spend some time discussing, I will admit at first, various GWR topics, notably the gas-turbine No. 18000 and Mr Hawksworth.. At some stage the conversation turned to the Southern and Mr Bulleid - it was Paul who recalled the story of how in the Brighton drawing office during the rush to complete the design work on 'Leader' that Bulleid had torn a strip off the senior draftsman for daring to suggest a modification to the drive to the sleeve valves, notwithstanding the fact that a demonstration of how a desk drawer would jam if pushed back with pressure just on one side. (We all know the sleeves did jam in practice as well, what was being suggested was a drive to adopt a 'push-pull' movement.)

There the conversation ended until a second encounter more recently and again at an exhibition. Once more

Whilst there are numerous illustrations of the BR 4MT design available, it was only right that we include those taken by Paul to illustrate the point made. Here with the 'tumblehome' clearly visible is No. 80151 facing the Isle of Wight at Lymington Pier having arrived with a railtour on 9 April 1967.

ANOTHER BULLEID ENIGMA?

Have you ever seen such a filthy and unkempt machine? Reported to be No. 80140 at Clapham Junction with the 'Kenny Belle' on 23 May 1967. Notwithstanding its external condition the engine managed to survive at Nine Elms until the very end.
Paul Russenberger

the topic turned to Mr Bulleid and this time his influence upon the design of one of the BR Standard types.

To put this in context we must first ask how much, if anything, the BR Standard types owed to the influence of Mr Bulleid? Probably little, but then Paul came up with what is such an obvious comment, I and I suspect many others will have missed in the past. "Look at the profile of the side tanks on the 4MT", Paul commented, "It matches exactly the profile of a Bulleid coach - as does the tender profile of the Q1 and tender of the Bulleid Pacifics." And where was much of the design work for these engines completed? At Brighton. Likewise, where was much of the design work for the BR Class 4 tanks completed? Again at Brighton. (Brighton may have been responsible for the 'crease' in the cab sides joining two surfaces on the BR standard engines. We all know the general design work was shared between a number of offices.)

So we ask the next question: was such a profile necessary on the 2-6-4T to suit the loading gauge and here the answer is that it was not. The conclusion then is simple, the Bulleid influence did continue, perhaps not in true me-

chanical form but certainly from an aesthetic perspective. Paul is of the opinion that Brighton may have quietly slipped the Bulleid profile into the drawings and got it through without anyone noticing until it was too late! (Somewhere I have read it was at one time believed the BR Class 4 tanks were also to be fitted with BFB wheels, again the Brighton influence. I thought this was in Sean Day-Lewis biography on Bulleid or an issue of the 'R.O' but cannot now locate the reference. Possibly such a design step was too radical. But with a considerable number of the 80xxx series engines destined to work on the Southern Region, a modification to the profile may well have been officially approved. Even so it would have taken far more work to produce such curvature compared with a simple vertical form. I can see many readers reaching for their various books to compare photographs. If you do look at the Fairburn type, the other BR Standard types, tank and tender and the comparisons will be immediately obvious.)

Well done Mr Bulleid, well done Brighton, (and of course well done Paul). One up I think to the Southern!

SOUTHERN RAILWAY STEAM BREAKDOWN CRANES

Part 1 Inherited Cranes

Peter Tatlow

London & South Western Railway

When the Southern Railway was established it inherited from its constituents ten steam breakdown cranes. The biggest contributor was of course the largest, the London & South Western Railway with seven. It had been early in the field with this class of equipment, being second only to the Midland Railway, in investing in steam-powered breakdown cranes, when in 1875 it acquired a 10-ton crane from the early crane maker Appleby Bros, followed by another five years later.

Their third acquisition was from the firm of Dunlop & Bell of Liverpool in 1885 who supplied a 15 ton crane again on three axles. As No 1, this was first posted to Nine Elms depot, where, as well as breakdown work, it was also used for handling boilers in the Works yard. Its arrival will have probably displaced one of the Appleby 10-ton cranes. By 1896, the two Appleby cranes were allocated to Northam (No 3) and Exmouth Jct (No 2).

Twenty years later, when on 1 July 1905, the disaster at Salisbury occurred, these three cranes were the LSWR's total steam breakdown crane capacity available to clear the debris. At this time in history one can only conjecture how these small cranes managed to handle the heavy loads involved. Their struggle to achieve the task must have prompted Dugald Drummond to place an order for the next batch of two 20-ton cranes from Stothert & Pitt of Bath, which were delivered in 1908 and 1909. The new No 1 was sent to Nine Elms, while the second crane No 5 was despatched Exmouth Jct., thereby allowing the 15-ton crane at Nine Elms, now No 3, to be sent to Eastleigh and 10-ton No 2 to go to Guildford. Appleby crane No 4, formerly No 3, disappeared in 1925, while No 2 struggled on until it suffered an accident to its jib when it came in contact with an over-bridge in Guildford Yard on 26 March 1934 and was subsequently withdrawn.

Impressed by the 36-ton long jib cranes supplied at the same period to the Great Western and LNWR, together with the increasing size and weight of locomotives he was introducing, led Robert Urie to place an order with Ransomes & Rapier of Ipswich in early 1915 for a similar crane. The pressures of war, however, meant that this was not delivered until 1918, when as No 6 it displaced the 20-ton crane from Nine Elms to Eastleigh in turn releasing the 15 ton to go to Salisbury, while the 10-ton there turned up at Bournemouth.

When, however, the LSWR sought to repeat the order, it would appear that the delivery period and / or cost led the work to be placed with Cowans Sheldon of Carlisle, instead of Ransomes & Rapier, who supplied a crane to the same performance specification. No 7 went to Salisbury enabling the 15-ton crane there to be despatched to Feltham.

London, Brighton & South Coast Railway .

During the 1890s many railway companies were acquiring 15-ton steam cranes of a standard design from Cowans & Sheldon, including the LBSC which invested in two with a swan-neck jib in 1898. Posted to each end of the main line they took up residence for the next thirty years at Brighton and New Cross as Nos 16 and 17.

South Eastern Railway

Shortly before the inauguration of the working agreement between the SER and LC&DR in 1899, the former had ordered a single example of Cowans Sheldon's standard product of 15 ton crane. This was stationed at their main works in Ashford for nearly thirty years, when it was replaced by an LBSC example and went to Stewarts Lane.

Part 2, covering **SR CRANES** will be published in 2013 to coincide with the second part of Peter's book on **'RAILWAY BREAKDOWN CRANES'**

Opposite top - *LSWR 's 10-ton Appleby steam breakdown 6-wheeled crane No 4 at Strawberry Hill on 25 June 1921, having become de-railed in the yard. (HC Casserley [863])*

Opposite bottom - *A view of the LSWR's 15-ton Dunlop & Bell crane No 1 at Nine Elms in 1890. (BR, author's collection)*

The author of the recently published *Railway Breakdown Cranes - Volume 1,* Peter Tatlow discusses those cranes that came into the hands of the SR.

Top - *The ex-LSWR's 20-ton steam crane, supplied by Stothert & Pitt in 1909, seen at Feltham on 5 March 1963 as No Ds 34, shortly before its withdrawal. (TM Abbott [3813/484])*

Bottom - *The two LSWR 36-ton cranes, Ransomes & Rapier No Ds35 from Eastleigh nearest the camera and Cowans Sheldon No Ds37 attend to derailed 2-6-0 N Class No 31816 at Tipton Yard, Eastleigh during the afternoon of 19 November 1962. (TM Abbott [A/2])*

Opposite top - *An example of Cowans Sheldon's standard 15-ton crane is ex-SER crane No L3, now SR No 202S, as it clears debris the day after the collision at Swanley Jct. on 27 June 1937. (HC Casserley [14305])*

Steam Breakdown Cranes Inherited by the Southern Railway

Capacity/ Purchased by	Maker	Wheel arrang.	Date del'd	Running No.		Match wagon No.		Allocation	Disposal
				Pre-group	SR/BR	Pre-group	SR/BR		
10T / LSWR	Appleby	0-6-0	1875	3, later 4	33S	63S	33SM	Northam '96, Eastleigh 1/03, Salisbury *1/1/11*, Strawberry Hill *25/7/21*. Bournemouth *'22-'23*, Ashford (K) 1/12/24	Wdn 1925
10T / LSWR	Appleby	0-6-0	1880	2	31S	8809	31SM	Exmouth Jct. *'96-'05*, Guildford *1/1/11-26/3/34*	Wdn. 31/11/34
15T / LSWR	Dunlop & Bell	0-6-0	1885	1, later 3	32S	(i) 70S (ii) 57450	(i & ii) 32SM	Nine Elms *c'95/6*, Eastleigh 1/1/11, Salisbury *25/7/21*, Feltham *'22-'23*, Bournemouth Central 1/12/24	Wdn. 27/4/46
20T / LSWR	Stothert & Pitt	0-4-4	1908	1	30S / Ds30	885	30SM / Ds??	Nine Elms '08-*1/1/11*, Eastleigh *25/7/21-10/5/40*, Bournemouth 4/46	Wdn. 8/6/63
20T / LSWR	Stothert & Pitt	0-4-4	1909	5	34S / Ds34	895	34SM / Ds3082	Exmouth Jct '09-*10/5/40*, Feltham *4/46-5/3/63*	Wdn. 17/5/63
36T / LSWR	Ransomes & Rapier	0-6-4	1918	6	35S / Ds35	67S+68S	35SM+34 SM Ds3083+ Ds3084	Nine Elms '18-*7/37*, Fratton *5/38-6/46*, Eastleigh *11/47-1/7/49*	Wdn. 9/1/65
36T / LSWR	Cowans Sheldon	0-6-4	1922	7	37S / Ds37 WR376	115S+116S	37SM+38 SM / Ds3085+ Ds3086	Salisbury '22-*10/5/40*, Exmouth Jct. (tempy) 7/44, Salisbury *'47-10/67*, WR 7/67, Worcester *10/67-'70*, Landore *12/9/70*	Wdn. '71
15T / LBSCR	Cowans Sheldon	0-6-4	1898	16	315S / Ds315		315SM	Brighton, Ashford (K) - *26/3/34*, Stewart's Lane *25/8/50-1/5/63*	Wdn. 23/2/63
15T / LBSCR	Cowans Sheldon	4-4-0	1898	17	316S / Ds316		(1) 316SM (2) Ds22426	New Cross Gate *26/3/34-44*, Stewart's Lane *25/8/50-1/5/63*	Wdn. 9/3/63
15T / SECR	Cowans Sheldon	4-4-0	1899	L3	202S / Ds202		(1) 4747 (2) 202SM Ds3089	Ashford (K) '00, Stewart's Lane *26/3/34-7/49*, Gillingham (K) *24/52-3/5/59*	Wdn. 3/11/62

Note: The dates it is thought a crane was first allocated to a depot are shown in upright letters. Where a crane is merely known to have been at a depot on a specific date(s) they are shown in italics.

Left - The Author at Bournemouth West circa 1950: final destination of the Brighton – Bournemouth – the West Terminus. Here a young Bill Allen gazes towards the buffer stops. In the background a Drummond M7 and one of the local pilots – an Adams O2 No.212 still in SR livery some time after 1948. This engine was allocated post-war to Bournemouth and employed mainly on shunting turns until transfer to Eastleigh in November 1956, it was withdrawn in 1959. The mainland O2's retained original smaller bunkers compared with the extended version on the Isle of Wight locomotives. No. 212 also retained an original Adams boiler and boiler fittings. The M7 is push-pull fitted and no doubt used on the "Ringwood line"– Castleman's Corkscrew as it was known.

SOUTH COAST STEAM

Bill Allen

A sunny summer Sunday in Sussex! The year is 1954 or '55 and an excited throng of day trippers wait on platform 2 at Barnham station. Most have travelled up the short branch line from Bognor Regis on the 10.07am and others have congregated from the villages around Barnham. Very few have travelled by car - local buses would have been the most likely connection or simple walking. People of all ages are looking forward to a day out in Bournemouth. It seems strange that, living in a seaside resort, Bognor, which itself will be teeming with day visitors from London and the suburbs, that they should choose to travel some 65 miles along the south coast to another, albeit bigger and more sophisticated, town. But once there the different pleasures of cliffs, funicular railway down the cliff from Bournemouth West station and the wide golden sands will mean a good day out and an adventure for young and old.

And what train do they await? The 10 o'clock which has started its journey from Brighton, calling at Worthing Central 10.19am, Barnham 10.39am, Chichester 10.50am, Havant 11.3am, before continuing on to Bournemouth with stops at Southampton Central 11.42am, Brockenhurst 12.5pm Bournemouth Central 12.30pm and Bournemouth West, arriving at its destination at 12.42pm.

But for your author only just into double figures in years the excitement is greater because in this electrified area of the Southern Region the Brighton to Bournemouth is steam-hauled! One of three trains from Brighton daily in summer to Bournemouth, Plymouth and Cardiff which leave the electrified line just after Havant.

So picture the scene: looking due east the track is on a slight fall into Barnham station. In the middle distance a double semaphore signal guards access to platforms 1 and 2. As the due arrival time approaches the first indication of the train is the signal rising. The train has the road for plat-

form 2. Tension rises as eyes are strained to the horizon for the first sight of a column of steam indicating the imminent arrival of the train. And here it is; regulator eased, brakes on and a Brighton Atlantic passes the crowds to draw to a stop near the starter and signal box. The passengers open the doors of the Maunsell or Bulleid carriages and struggle in with picnic hampers, buckets and spades, push chairs and small children to try and find seats in the already well-filled train. A wave from the Guard and *Trevose Head* eases away effortlessly from the station. Today's adventure has begun.

In this article I will describe a little of the history of the South Coast services, concentrating on the 50s and 60s which was my direct experience. In fact travelling to school every day from Bognor to Chichester on the routine school train that ran in the mornings and afternoons, I often took the opportunity of using the Bournemouth- Brighton return service to get an opportunity to travel on a steam train. The returning school service was at 4.10pm and consisted usually of 2x2 emu units (2-BILs); one pair allocated to the Girls High School and the other pair allocated to the Boys High School - needless to say with no corridor connection between the two! The Bournemouth to Brighton train used to arrive about five to ten minutes before this service and when one had reached the elevated heights of the sixth form one could use this train as an alternative to the school service. Chichester was often used to take water from the crane at the end of the platform before the last leg of the journey on to Brighton.

Genesis: The 1912 LBSCR timetable shows that a service along the coast had been running for a long time. A through train departed from Brighton at 11.20am with through coaches to Salisbury and on to Plymouth. The train itself ran to Bournemouth. During the Second World War the Plymouth to Brighton continued, presumably well pa-

Opposite, middle - No. 34046 coasts into Chichester on the last leg of the journey to Brighton with original cab and high-sided tender. The first coach is a Maunsell Brake Second. Directly behind the train is the turning triangle leading into the Cathedral fields. This was needed to enable locos on in-coming freights to be turned ready for return journeys. There was a turntable at Bognor shed but this would have necessitated a light engine movement. The scene is completely transformed today with a Waitrose super-store, car park and leisure centre replacing the sylvan fields. In the foreground coal wagons sit reminding us of the domestic fuel and gas works requirements in the post war era – to say nothing of the appetite of steam engines! No. 34046 Braunton was a long term 75A engine. New to traffic on 14 November 1946 it arrived at Brighton in June 1951 and stayed until January 1959 when called to Eastleigh for rebuilding. After this it was allocated to Bournemouth. Withdrawn in October 1965 she was saved for preservation via Woodhams and is still extant and running.

Opposite, bottom - The lower photograph is something different. When I looked at the negatives I thought we had different views of the same train approaching Chichester – but no this shot shows another West Country but with extended smoke deflectors The give away is of course the stock with a plum and spilt milk vehicle at the head of the train.

Departure from Barnham. No. 34045 'Ottery St Mary' quietly gets away from Barnham westward bound on a Brighton coast service. While the Bulleids had a reputation for slipping I do not remember many such events here – perhaps the reason might be a combination of fairly light load and lack of deposits of oil on the rails as so few steam traversed this route. The contrast was to watch departures at Basingstoke or Salisbury when the pyrotechnics and symphony of spinning wheels, motion and steam was something to behold! No. 34045 is in commendably clean condition with a late crest. The line to Bognor branches off to the left. This was an important junction – the 12 coach Victoria electrics joined here. In practice a 4-COR and 4-BUF would arrive from Bognor first followed by a 4-COR from Portsmouth Harbour. Our morning school train used the cross-over in the foreground to reverse from Bognor en route to Chichester.

tronised by service personnel on leave or posting from Naval Bases in Plymouth and the Army on Salisbury Plain. The December 1944 'Railway Observer' describes "The Plymouth – Brighton train arrived in Brighton on the 4th November hauled by N class 1875 from Eastleigh shed". At that time this was an Eastleigh duty but normally with a Drummond 4-4-0. The timetable at that time showed the train departing from Brighton at 11.45am proceeding to Romsey where the 12.55pm Portsmouth and Southsea combined. In later years a similar joining happened at Fareham.

Still in Malachite green, sister engine No. 34037, 'Clovelly' leaves Barnham in Easter week 1949 on a South Coast Express. She has the wedge shaped cab fitted the month before, visibility forward was improved by this modification but drifting steam from the soft exhaust was never fully successfully solved despite many variations in smoke deflectors.

No. 34059 'Sir Archibald Sinclair. at Salisbury. Westward bound from platform 4 at Salisbury is Battle of Britain No. 34059. This platform was used for main line trains taking the former LSWR route to the West. In the bay, platform 5, some Maunsell stock awaits departure on a stopper to Exeter or Yeovil. Repairs / re-decorations to the canopy are in hand from the scaffolding seen. Salisbury was outside the 'Holiday Runabout' ticket Mike Hudson and I purchased each summer for our train spotting. But if we chose a stopping train from Southampton Central to Salisbury we knew the stock would be non-corridor – so no chance of travelling ticket inspectors or a nosy guard! On arrival a parcel exit gate not far from where this photo was taken could surreptitiously be used to leave the platform. Once outside a 1d platform ticket allowed access to this busy station. Departure back was simply a reversal of the process – no-one missed two boys from the platform!

After the end of the war the October timetable announced the introduction of through trains to Bournemouth and Cardiff to join the Plymouth. The timings remained the same well into BR days: 9.40am to Bournemouth, 11.0am to Cardiff and 11.30am to Plymouth. To quote the 'Railway Observer' again, "The Bournemouth train is usually worked by 430 (a L12), the Cardiff train which takes the timing of the previous 11.0am Plymouth is worked by an Eastleigh D15, while the Plymouth, put back to 11.30am, is worked by 423 or 428 (again L12s)." The L12s were transferred to Brighton specifically for these duties. The 'Railway Observer' records variations, with a B4X, No. 2056, on the Bournemouth and T9 No. 312 on the Plymouth. Eastleigh substituted T9s and L12s for the D15 occasionally but unusually a smaller wheeled S11, No. 400 was used on 27/8/45. No. 400 as 30400 was the last survivor of the class when finally withdrawn from Guildford in the autumn of 1954 having outlived fellow class members by three years. B4Xs did appear on an irregular basis in 1946 but exceptionally on 18th March the 'Railway Observer' reported that all these trains were hauled by "Greybacks" – No.2067 on the Bournemouth, No.2043 on the Cardiff and No. 2045 on the Plymouth. This latter locomotive was fitted with a Drummond chimney.

With Bulleid light Pacifics emerging monthly from Brighton works it seems strange that more opportunity wasn't taken to use the coast trains to provide a hard running-in turn. No. 21C135 was used on the Plymouth returning on the Cardiff for two days in August. This was the second occasion that a 'West Country' was used (the 'Railway Observer' does not report the first case). So the coast line saw a class for the first time which was to become so familiar in the years to come. In September No. 21C137 *Clovelly* made her first appearance. Another debutante on the coast trains was No. 928 *Stowe*, the first time a 'Schools' class had been seen. No. 929 was also used and a typical run is quoted in the 'Observer'. "*Malvern* hauled the Plymouth, 205 tons behind the tender, until the Portsmouth portion was added at Fareham when the train increased in load to 380 tons." While time was lost on this run due to the plethora of speed restrictions, the 'Railway Observer' says that "the use of these engines has considerably improved the running between Brighton and Fareham and enabled the piloting between Fareham and Southampton Central to be discontinued."

A change in shed responsibilities occurred in Spring 1947. Salisbury took over the Plymouth arriving in Brighton on the return train, stabling overnight and returning to Salisbury the following morning on the Plymouth. This saw the first regular use of the Bulleids – No. 21C153 on 29 April for example. On Saturday only the sole 'Schools' now left at Brighton, No. 930 *Radley* was used. (Nos. 928/9 had been transferred to St Leonards). After a period out of the timetables the Bournemouth was restored in the summer of 1947 but only on Saturdays. The 'Railway Observer' records that on the first day (21/6/47) the train consisted of 8 coaches with B4X No. 2073 at the head. No. 930 appeared in July instead of the usual loco. for the Saturday-only Plymouth. The 'Schools' Class did not reappear regularly at Brighton again until the late 50s.

Summer and Nationalisation in 1948 saw the end for the B4Xs with H1s used on the Bournemouth and the reinstatement of the three routes meant an opportunity to allocate three West Country Bulleid Pacifics to Brighton for the services. These initial three were Nos. 21C133-35 (34033-5) and with their arrival Salisbury lost the Brighton – Plymouth roster. 1949 saw the allocation of 'West Countries' increase to four with Nos. 21C137-40 (34037-40). By the

Ardingly at Salisbury: Schools No. 30917 'Ardingly' off shed at Salisbury and at the east end of the station to be in position to take over either the Plymouth or Cardiff – Brighton. The timescale is the late 50's or early 60's. No. 30917 was a long-term Ramsgate 73G engine until the Kent Coast electrification made steam redundant. Allocation to Brighton was from July 1959. This roster, taking over from a WR Hall, Grange or County on the Cardiff, or a Bulleid on the Plymouth, would normally have been for a Brighton West Country. No. 30917 has the Bulleid modification of Lemaitre blast pipe and large diameter chimney. The engine was withdrawn in November 1962.

summer of that year loads were increasing – cross country leisure travel and holidays were picking up even at this time of austerity. The increase in public usage meant once again that particularly the Plymouth loaded to a maximum of 10 coaches and included a Buffet Car.

It is useful to realise that while the routes were not too arduous in gradient terms, Fareham – St Denys included Swanwick bank 1 in 70 up in the Southampton direction and 1 in 81 in the reverse and this combined with a tortuous course around Southampton with speed restrictions added to the work demanded of the engine. Brighton to Havant was basically level after a gentle six miles downhill at 1-264 from Brighton to Shoreham. After the diversion of the Salisbury line at Redbridge, Southampton to Bournemouth was an up and down route through the New Forest before a sustained downhill through Hinton Admiral (a scene of some speeds in the final days of steam). Then the line rose a little from Christchurch to Boscombe and on to Bournemouth. The Salisbury line rose gently through Romsey, Dundridge and Dean before falling to Milford Junction and Salisbury tunnel.

The arrival of powerful new Pacifics should have transformed Brighton MPD's (75A) approach to the South Coast services. Sadly as we shall see availability was never a constant and failures, substitutions and an actual decision to allocate other locomotives to the rosters was the pattern to come through the 50s and 60s. By 1950 D15s had also completely disappeared from the trains, (banned between Havant

and Angmering for some reason unknown to the author). The Brighton Atlantics (H1s and H2s) had made occasional trips on the Bournemouth. The H1s were near their end – No. 32039 was the last at 75A and was withdrawn in December. The H2s came in and out of store at Newhaven each winter but often worked to Bournemouth in 1950, when a 'West Country' was not available. Austerity and rationing was still severe and all the Brighton South Coast trains were withdrawn in January 1951 as an economy measure.

But for the summer of 1951 the trains were reinstated – however in advance of this Southern Region made a decision to send all the Pacifics away from Brighton – No. 34039 gained celebrity by being re-allocated briefly to Stratford on the GE section of the Eastern Region – Nos. 34037/38 went to Plymouth and Nos. 34040/41 to Bath for Somerset and Dorset services. The plan was to use Maunsell 3-cylinder U1 2-6-0s and Fairburn LMS design 2-6-4Ts (being built at Brighton works at that time). In the future both the Fairburns and the later BR Standard 2-6-4Ts appeared spasmodically on the South Coast trains. Water was routinely taken by all locos rostered to the services at Chichester and Southampton Central – thereby meaning no problem was experienced with water capacity with the tank engines. Apparently no difficulty appeared to occur with the reduced coal capacity. Brighton sent out Atlantics on the Bournemouth but clearly the loss of Pacifics was keenly felt and "Control" was forced to rescind the decision regarding the Pacifics which was reversed. Nos. 34045 – 48 were allocated joined by No. 34039 back from her Eastern Escapade in March 1952.

So the locomotives I best recall had arrived: No. 34039 *Boscastle*, No. 34045 *Ottery St Mary*, No. 34046 *Braunton*, No. 34047 *Callington* and No. 34048 *Crediton*. The 'Railway Observer' comments "The through trains from Brighton over the Netley line have not been hauled by 2-6-4Ts for some weeks, 34045-7 have been used and keep much better time than the tanks" And later in December issue "32422 ex-store was 3 minutes early with 9 coaches and a van on the Brighton – Plymouth. This excellent performance compares very well with the indifferent performance of the 2-6-4Ts" Clearly the experiment had failed and 'West Countries' and H2s re-established an ascendancy that was to continue for some time.

But on the other side of the coin the early fifties started a history of poor availability of the Bulleids. 1952 showed how reliable the H2s were in contrast. Autumn that year saw No. 32421 (*South Foreland*) used on the Bournemouth regularly. Shed staff at 75A bestowed the nickname 'Old Faithful' on her and her performance and economy (compared with the more profligate Pacifics) increased her popularity with the enginemen rostered to her. The

'Railway Observer' reports that "amazingly 32421 was officially in store"! All sorts of locomotives were seconded to substitute for failures. En route and at destinations a failure meant a local replacement that would complete the turn and run the train the following day – when hopefully fitters from the away shed would have cured the problem Bulleid. So The 'Railway Observer' again reports "L12 30415, N 31805, Standard and Fairburn tanks, D15 30470 (presumably allowed through to Brighton) and even a D1 31735 0n the Plymouth". Interestingly No. 34045 had disgraced itself by derailing at Brighton station and I suppose the nearest replacement was rapidly grabbed. The D1 was itself substituted at Southampton Central by a Standard 2-6-2T 82012 for the relatively short run to Salisbury – nevertheless quite a task for a modest tank. No doubt the D1 returned to Brighton to resume its correct diagram later. Drummond T9s also were frequent substitutes from Bournemouth, Eastleigh and Salisbury.

This pattern of problems continued in Coronation Year 1953. 75A must have been a nightmare shed to work at with poor availability of their premier locomotives, the 'West Countries' and the ageing H2s that themselves lacked their previous reliability. But suffice to say they were considered a better option for the Bournemouths and were offi-

No. 10000 at Southampton: En route between Brighton and Bournemouth was Southampton Central where we train spotters disembarked late morning and took up our places at the London end to watch the comings and goings. On this sunny day in 1954, 10000 (one of the LMS diesels) was awaiting departure to Waterloo. The two boys look on in some amazement at the locomotive, little knowing probably that they were looking at the pioneer of future motive power on British Railways. 10000 was based at Nine Elms from March 1953 to April 1955. With her twin 10001 and the three SR diesels Nos. 10201-03, they took their turns on the major trains between Waterloo and Bournemouth and Exeter. All were dispatched to the LMR by 1955.

No. 21C150, later to be named 'Royal Observer Corps' at Barnham around the end of 1947 on the Plymouth – Brighton. At this time the Salisbury roster brought a Bulleid on this train. In the distance is the slight rise towards Yapton and Ford Junction. In somewhat disreputable condition for a new engine, some wag has added a scrawl on the air-smoothed side, which I think reads "Sexy Moira" – I wonder who Moira was and whether she knew she was temporarily immortalised on a railway engine! (The mind boggles!)

cially rostered to the trains in the winter diagrams. In 1953 another new class made a first appearance on the South Coast – Standard 76xxx 2-6-0s. Nos. 76010/17 as substitutes – allocated to Eastleigh the class made regular appearances through the fifties on a new Summer only service from Romsey to Littlehampton. Arriving in Littlehampton at 10.53am the locomotive concerned went to Bognor Shed for turning and engine requirements before departing at 6.30pm for the return journey, the day trippers no doubt having enjoyed the delights of the South Coast resort.

In our chronological tour of the South Coast expresses, 1954/55 marked my arrival on the "train-spotting" scene and in both years H2s were well to the fore. The 'Railway Observer' said that while the rosters list WCs, "doubtless the Atlantics will deputise on one or more of their duties each week". And Standard 2-6-4Ts also appeared again "reports speeds touching 75mph between Worthing and Ford – an unusual speed over the line". D Fereday Glenn in an article he wrote in the January 1980 'Railway World' makes reference to "Sometimes a shortage of 4-6-2s at Brighton (not unusual) might result in a whole variety of substitutes......I have heard tales of such rarities as a Wainwright D 4-4-0". In correspondence I made at the

time I said "I can confirm that a 'D' did appear on at least one occasion to the fascination of those less well versed in railway matters who were amazed that such a venerable looking machine should be used on what was apparently an express service". The 'Railway Observer' doesn't confirm my observation but it certainly reminds us that equally elderly albeit perhaps more sprightly pensioners in the T9s were seen and as with the D1 incident often 75A would simply take a loco off another visiting roster and use it.

But 1956 dawned with ominous signs for the Marsh Atlantics – stored through the winter months once again at Newhaven Shed. None were steamed between 25th January and 9th March. In June Nos. 32421 and 32424 joined No. 32425 at 75A. No. 32425 had made an early fleeting appearance on the Bournemouth on 1st June. It is appropriate to retell the events of that year through a quotation from the 'Railway Observer'. "All the H2s had their bogies removed for examination all except *Beachy Head* had them replaced but the locos did no work and were out of traffic" – a fracture on LNER No. 60700 had caused a need for this as the H2s had a similar design of bogie reminding us of a certain common parentage of the Ivatt, Marsh and Gresley designs. The August edition worsened the story: "It

Salisbury with a D15. Post-war, D15's had an Eastleigh duty on the Brighton south coast trains so here is No. 30470 at Salisbury in early BR days, perhaps 1949/50. Your author is in the foreground age 6 or 7. (While scanning the negative for this article I realised that I could, (a), read the number of the loco and (b, was present when the photo was taken.........so a quick re-visit to the appropriate Ian Allan and an underline to No. 30470 as a very belated 60 year on "cop"!) The engine is on a Salisbury – Portsmouth service, the front coaches of GWR origin / design which quickly identifies it as an inter-region working from Bristol or Cardiff. No. 30470 was withdrawn in December 1952, one of the more successful 4-4-0s that Dugald Drummond designed.

is understood that serious defects were discovered in 32421/26 and as a result it had been decided to scrap both. And 32422 was confined to light duties only and likely to go before the end of 1956. This is sad news for their many admirers, the more so as they were not programmed for withdrawal in 1956 or 1957".

The death knell had rung and while the survivors made appearances on the Bournemouth only *Beachy Head* survived the year and was occasionally used on Duty 730 (the Bournemouth) which was still programmed for a H2. Even No. 32425 was withdrawn despite

being in good condition. The loss of the Atlantics left a void that was filled by the transfer from Ashford (74A) in early 1957 of Ls Nos. 31776-8. These Wainwright 4-4-0s had been excellent, successful locomotives in Kent and East Sussex for many years and while they too were on less demanding duties than in their heyday, were well received by Brighton. The Ls were frequently used on the Bournemouth and were extremely popular with the crews according to the 'Railway Observer'. "31777 successfully managed the Brighton – Cardiff with a winter load of 8 coaches with exemplary timekeeping". This makes an interesting contrast

The U1s appeared occasionally on the Brighton South Coast trains as substitutes for Bulleids or the Atlantics. This view of No. 1897 is taken at Bognor, the loco departing with a freight train in early BR days. Note the 'SOUTHERN' struck through with a line on the tender. As No. 31897 it was allocated to Redhill for much of the late 40s and 50s and survived until 1962.

with a "press-ganged" appearance of No. 31776 on 19th December 1956 on the Plymouth – always the heaviest loaded train and full no doubt pre-Christmas. The booked 'West Country' had again derailed outside Brighton station. The 12 coach train was too much for the L which stalled on Swanwick Bank and No. 76018 had to be summoned to the train to assist. The Ls stayed at 75A until June 1959 when they were transferred to Nine Elms to end their days.

Through all these changes No. 32424 was still in use but fragile – failing twice including blowing out the front end of her left hand cylinder. She survived to be repaired and exhibited at Eastleigh Works Open Day on 7th August 1957 (see photo accompanying the article). She re-entered traffic to work duties from 75A that autumn but was soon out of use again. After a winter in store *Beachy Head* re-emerged to work a RCTS special on 13th April before the end came. Attempts to preserve failed; but how appropriate that on the Bluebell a recreation, phoenix-like of a duplicate *Beachy Head* is in hand....but that's another story albeit one well worth supporting financially. So an era on the South Coast Services had ended – the graceful, Edwardian lines of the Marsh Atlantics were missed by everyone.

The start of 1958 saw the Ls in regular use on the Bournemouth and the 'West Country's on the Plymouth and Cardiff. Summer saw extra relief trains run – 7.49am Bristol – Brighton and 10.00am SO relief Brighton to Cardiff. But rather surprisingly the Bournemouth on Sundays was re-timed to run to the weekday timetable i.e. back early afternoon and therefore not much use to the day trippers we saw at the start of the article! And the summer also saw the arrival of an allocation of Schools V 4-4-0s. Immediately post-war Brighton had used Vs on the through trains and the 'Railway Observer' says "It is pleasant to see them appearing again". This new strand to the passenger locomotive strength came as a result of the Kent Coast electrification.

Redundant on the trains to Hastings, Dover and Margate the highly competent Maunsell 'Schools' class were a welcome addition, arriving first with Nos. 30900/01 in 1958. Four more Nos. 30914/15 and 30916/17 joined the allocation which meant six strong passenger locomotives were there to alleviate some of the chronic difficulties at Brighton. The latter-day history of the 'Schools' at Brighton is well covered by Jeffrey Grayer's recent article in Issue 13 of Southern Way. Suffice to say that 4-4-0s replacing 4-6-2s on not just the Bournemouth but also the Plymouth and Cardiff seems strange until you look at the appalling availability of the Bulleids at Brighton.

Modern, powerful and in respectable condition, the 'Schools' quickly became regular performers on the Bournemouth and Salisbury turns. They also had their reliability problems however – was it something that locomotives allocated to 75A were prone to? So Ls were still in evidence until the winter services of 1958. Coupled with these new arrivals were changes to the allocation of Bulleids. All the old 'favourites' departed, Nos. 34045/47 to Eastleigh to be modified and then joined by Nos. 34039/46/48. Nos.34008/19 arrived with Nos. 34097-9. Despite these changes fears were emerging that all these popular cross-country trains would be withdrawn as an economy measure. But this was a palpably wrong proposal and the effect would have been to cause even more overcrowding on the newly- introduced Hampshire Diesel Multiple Units; to say nothing of the more tortuous journey. Brighton to Bournemouth would have required an EMU to Fratton – change and lugging suitcases, pushchairs and children over a footbridge to join a DEMU. No doubt a wait would ensue and then another change at Southampton Central to await a Waterloo – Bournemouth express!

But 1959 started with yet another suspension of the Bournemouth as an economy measure. The service recommenced in the summer and was practically monopolised by 'Schools' Nos. 30900/1/14 & 15. The 'Schools' also were used on the Salisbury trains joining the newly arrived Bulleids. In September No. 30917 joined the stud at 75A meaning there were five Pacifics and six 'Schools' for four (three in winter) top link duties! But maintenance levels were reported to be lower than ever with engines out of service for long periods! 1960 saw the beginning of the end of steam on the South Coast Services. Initially little changed although transfers and re-allocations saw Nos. 34038/57 arrive from Exmouth Junction (72A) (to replace Nos. 34097/8) – both locomotives had high reputations in the West but one wonders how they fared at 75A! For No. 34038 *Lynton* it was a return to old haunts nearly ten years are leaving in 1951. Her stay was brief, however, departing to Eastleigh in November 1961. No. 34008 came as the first modified Bulleid to be at Brighton. Vs Nos. 30902/18/19 from 70A joined as others departed to Redhill.

Christmas chaos on the 6th December was reported by the 'Railway Observer' – "The Plymouth – Brighton reached Shoreham and the crew discovered that the tender was empty of water! Attempts were made to top up with a hosepipe failed so the fire had to be thrown out setting fire to the sleepers which brought the local fire service into action. To compound the delays the fireman (engineman that is) dropped his shovel across the conductor rail short circuiting the track and chaos ensued. Electric trains were left isolated between stations and emergency bus services were put in place between Worthing and Brighton for some time." Shades of a pattern so familiar today in Network Rail days.

In 1961 attempts to improve the summer Bournemouth meant that apart from Saturdays the train was timetabled to make the return trip starting from Bournemouth at 6.35pm a much better time for day trippers. Yet come winter '61/'62 and the Bournemouth again was suspended. More excitement with the fire service happened with Battle of Britain *Biggin Hill* on the Bournemouth. The Bulleids were prone to fires under the air-smoothed casing and this occurred between Hamble and Netley. The Brigade dowsed the fire and No. 76019 took the train on to Bournemouth leaving No. 34057 in a siding smothered in foam. But arrival at Bournemouth was after the time the return should have departed. If the new timings were in place this must therefore have been a Saturday train. So Bournemouth commandeered a spare coaching set and No. 34046 *Braunton* made a return to old haunts although in rebuilt guise.

'Beachy Head': The classic lines of a Marsh Atlantic – at the Eastleigh Works Open Day in 1957. Already No. 32424 had been out of regular use for some time but managed to survive until 1958. I remember our surprise at finding her in the Works yard together with Adams 4-4-0 No 563. In the background the carriage works and sidings can be seen with the Eastleigh to Fareham line roughly central in the picture.

Cyclists Special at Chichester: My father and I were keen cyclist and members of Chichester Cycling Club. We often rode a tandem with me as 'stoker' and father as 'steersman'. The old station at Chichester has but months to live before modernisation will sweep away the narrow platforms, gas lamps, subway, dark dismal offices and waiting rooms. Today the rebuilt station still serves Chichester well. The bays were once used by Midhurst trains on the up side, on the downside for the all stations (and halts) Chichester to Portsmouth and Southsea trains – both now long gone. In the photograph No. 34092 'City of Wells' has arrived – your author, in a fetching belted two piece cycling outfit, is nearest the loco and we are ready to board. The Railway Observer of November 1956 says "Cyclists' Excursion: The Southern's first post-war venture in this field took place on 14 October when a special ran from East Croydon to Lyndhurst Road (in the New Forest) via Hove, Chichester and the Netley line. It was well supported by the Cycling Clubs of Surrey and Sussex and was full to capacity on leaving Chichester. The stock provided was four open seconds, a buffet car, and five vans."

In 1962 there was little of note to report. 'Schools' were still in use with Nos. 30901/17/28 in evidence. But once more 75A maintenance was at a low ebb and in early December, of the allocation of ten Bulleids, only two were in working order; so the Vs kept going until their premature demise at the end of the year. Also another class associated with the line at times, U1 No. 31903 was seen on the 5th December the last occasion when the three cylinder 2-6-0s were used. 1962 was the year the infamous decision to withdraw all remaining E6,K,& Vs for "accounting reasons" happened, irrespective of their condition.

The winter of 1962/3 proved to be one of the worst for years. Not since 1947 had so much snow fallen and the consequence was disruption to all services in the UK. For Brighton the combined effect of the snow and the inability of collieries to adequately maintain supplies of coal meant many cancellations of the South Coast trains. I was a dental student in London at that time and for a short spell had to commute from Bognor to Victoria in the 4-COR / 4-BUF express units then in use. Memory certainly confirms the cold mornings and evenings! A newcomer as an allocation at 75A was a Standard Class 5 4-6-0 – No. 73085 which was weight-restricted and used on the mainline and Salisbury turns. But this year, despite more Bulleids arriving, was

steam's swansong. The summer services still saw the Pacifics as the main motive power. The exception was the Bournemouth which was now diesel-hauled by Type 3 65XX's. In the autumn of 1963 all the 75A Pacifics were transferred away. Timetable changes and the arrival of the diesels accelerated their departure. The final allocation of Bulleids in September was Nos. 34012 *Launceston*, 34013 *Okehampton*, 34014 *Budleigh Salterton*, 34019 *Bideford*, 34027 *Taw Valley*, 34089 *602 Squadron*, and 34100 *Appledore* (all rebuilt) with Nos. 34055 *Fighter Pilot*, 34057 *Biggin Hill* and 34063 *229 Squadron* all in original unrebuilt condition. Exmouth Junction (72A) took over the Plymouth duty, coming to Brighton on the return service and returning to Exeter on the following morning on the 1130 to Plymouth. This diagram illustrated the maxim of using locomotives to maximum capacity for while at Brighton the loco was used on an evening freight to Norwood Junction and 5.32am Vans from London Bridge to Brighton. This alteration combined with the usual seasonal cancellation of the Bournemouth and Brighton to Cardiff was the precursor of a major alteration in early 1964.

Through trains on the Havant to Cosham line ceased. The Brighton – Plymouth was hauled to Portsmouth where the 72A Pacific took over having overnighted now at

Fratton MPD. Motive power on the Brighton – Portsmouth leg was the Raworth/Bulleid electric locomotives 20001-3. The Brighton to Cardiff was withdrawn becoming another Portsmouth to Cardiff train. The 'Railway Observer' notes that the last Bulleids on the services were seen on 4 & 5th January with Nos. 34070 and 34072 seen. But the magazine also notes that "despite the end of steam on the South Coast services a shortage of locomotives (at 75A again)meant that 34010 was borrowed from Nine Elms (70A) and used on the 11.0am Brighton – Portsmouth and 4.35pm return." And through the spring Standard 2-6-4T's reappeared on a number of occasions

Summer saw no return to the halcyon days. All steam services at 75A ended and the loss of facilities at Brighton meant that any "failures" that needed steam to work through to Brighton could not be serviced there! Laborious light engine movements to Redhill were made as a consequence. The Brighton – Cardiff was not re-instated, although a locally advertised "relief" was run in August to Cardiff, but without a balancing return trip! Types 3s were used. The evidence from the 'Railway Observer' demonstrates some indecisiveness and lack of consistency among the timetablers. So when winter arrived a retimed Plymouth exchanged locos from electric to steam at Chichester. The Pacifics continued via the direct line to Fareham again. Steam motive power was essential as the days grew colder because the Type 3s had no steam heating for the trains. The westbound exchange happened in the platform of the station but in the east direction as those who know Chichester will realise that successive busy level crossings and no provision of sidings meant a special stop was required at the home signal. Experience however found that the trains had difficulty keeping to time with this arrangement. So management abandoned this and a 72A Bulleid worked through to Brighton again returning light engine to Fratton.

1965 marked the end of our story of South Coast Steam. In June the Bournemouth train was re-instated but the comfortable Bulleid or Mark 1 steam stock was now a noisy modern 3-car Hampshire DEMU. Steam was banned on the Central Division and the remaining sheds at Redhill, Tunbridge Wells West and Eastbourne closed. Western Region DEMUs took over the Portsmouth – Bristol and Cardiff trains. The Brighton – Plymouth was diesel-hauled.

So a chapter of passenger trains that had served very well the communities in Sussex, Hampshire and counties west came to an end. Today EMUs travel the coast route to Southampton. Portsmouth-Bristol and Cardiff are in the hands of First Great Western Sprinters. But even now some glamour remains – A Brighton to Great Malvern train departs at 0900 and later in the day the 1700 departs for Worcester Shrub Hill. And No. 34067 *Tangmere* is occasionally seen raising the echoes through the houses on the outskirts of Chichester on special workings; reliving those days of the 50s and 60s.

Appendices: Sample Timetable and Locomotive Workings:

Some timetable facts as the Coast steam trains settled into BR days. By 1955, in the week the Brighton to Bournemouth ran to a timetable starting at 9.40am and arriving in Bournemouth at 12.22pm. And with a rapid turnround on Branksome shed the train returned at 1.50pm calling at Chichester at 4.03pm before arriving in Brighton at 4.54pm. But on Sundays in the summer the timetable changed to allow passengers to get a full afternoon's enjoyment at Bournemouth. Departure was much later at 7.32pm arriving in Chichester 9.12pm and for your author alighting at Barnham at 9.22pm to connect to Bognor arriving at 9.42pm. The train finally reached Brighton at 10.2pm. The end of a long day!

- Brighton – Cardiff departed Brighton at 11.0am, Barnham 11.38am, Chichester 11.49am arriving Cardiff 4.35pm

- Brighton - Plymouth Depart 11.30am, Barnham 12.5pm, Chichester 12.18pm, arriving Plymouth 6.11pm. Train includes a buffet car and added coaches from Portsmouth and Southsea at Fareham.

- The returning trips were Cardiff depart 12.50pm arriving Brighton 6.24pm, Plymouth 11.0am arriving Brighton 5.24pm

Locomotive Diagrams

Brighton MPD, 75A, was responsible for the supply of locomotives for the three coast steam services. Diagrams 730,731 & 732 on Monday to Saturday. Diagrams 732 & 733 on Sundays. Thus Brighton Diagram 732 on Sunday ran as follows:

7P/5F (WC)		732	
off 734	Saturdays		
---	Bricklayers Arms Loco (coupled to 633)	3.35am //	
3.50am	London Bridge	4.40am P	
5.43am	Brighton	7.55am //	
---	Brighton Loco	9.45am //	
**	Brighton	10.0am P	
1242pm	Bournemouth West	1.09pm //	
1.31pm	Bournemouth Central Loco	6.17pm //	
6.30pm	Bournemouth West	7.32pm P	
10.24pm	Brighton	** //	
**	Brighton Loco		

On Monday to Friday the diagram was

7P/5F (WC)		730	
---	Brighton Loco	9.25am //	
**	Brighton	9.40am P	
12.09am	Bournemouth Central	12.10pm //	

12.18pm	Branksome Loco	1.20pm //	
1.25pm	Bournemouth West Sidings	**	E Propel
**	Bournemouth West	1.50pm P	
4.54pm	Brighton	5.37pm E	
	(off 11.0am Plymouth)		
5.42pm	Hove	6.22pm //	

Except Weds 24/8 & Thurs 28/7,4/8, 18/8

6.30pm	Brighton Loco	---	

Weds 24/8 & Thurs 28/7,4/8,18/8

6.27pm	Preston Park	6.31pm E	
6.35pm	Brighton	** to Loco	

The reference on Sunday to "coupled to 633" was a Redhill N Class duty.

The locomotive was manned entirely by Brighton locomen as below in the week

1. No 1 P&D prepare loco

2. 1st set on 9.10am and work until 4.55pm

2nd set on 4.30pm, relieve at 4.55pm. Work and dispose. Then passenger 8.12pm to Lewes. Relieve No 760 at 8.39pm work and relieve.

Hence the Brighton men operate to and from Bournemouth including propelling the stock from Bournemouth West Sidings into the platform at the West station ready for the early afternoon return departure. Quite a hard onerous duty with only a break of an hour at Branksome to get some rest and a well deserved lunch.

The diagrams for the other two departures to Cardiff and Plymouth were as follows:

7P/5F		731	
---	Brighton Loco	10.45am //	
**	Brighton	11.00am P	
1.31pm	Salisbury	** //	
**	Salisbury Loco	2.30pm //	
**	Salisbury	2.55pm P	
	(11.10am ex Plymouth)		
5.24pm	Brighton	5.38pm //	
5.40pm	Brighton Loco	9.10pm F	

Fridays excepted

11.55pm	Norwood Yard	12.05am //	
12.20am	Norwood Loco	2.00am //	
2.30am	London Bridge	3.20am P	
4.32am	Brighton	6.15am //	
6.20am	Brighton Loco	---	

Fridays only

1155pm	Norwood Yard	2.00am //	

and as shown Saturdays

Once again one set of Brighton men sufficed for manning the loco from Brighton to Salisbury with again the statutory lunch hour for their "snap". Another handled the latter part of the diagram on the "Newspaper Train" London Bridge to Brighton.

Diagram 731 certainly utilised the locomotive to the full with only brief stays in Salisbury and Norwood for engine requirements

The final diagram is "The Plymouth", which included a Buffet car, was the heaviest working of the three.

7P/5F		732	

MO

---	Brighton Loco	11.15am //	
	(with Salisbury engine off 471 Sun)		
---	Brighton	11.30am P	
1.58pm	Salisbury	** //	
	Salisbury Loco	3.25pm //	
	(with Brighton engine off 733 Sun)		
	and as shown for MX		

MX

---	Brighton Loco	11.15am //	
**	Brighton	11.30am P	
1.58pm	Salisbury	** //	
---	Salisbury Loco	3.25pm //	
---	Salisbury	3.53pm P	
	(1.0pm ex Cardiff)		
6.24pm	Brighton	** //	
---	Brighton Loco	10.40pm //	
	(coupled to 733)		

FX

---	Brighton	11.18pm V	
	(double – head with 733 to E.Croydon)		
1.31am	London Bridge	1.45am //	
2.03am	Bricklayers Arms Loco	4.30am //	
	(coupled to 532)		
4.52am	London Bridge	5.32am V	
7.42am	Brighton	8.20am E	
**	Carriage Sidings	8.30am //	
**	Loco Yard	---	

FO

---	Brighton	11.18pm V	

(double-head with 733 to E.Croydon)

1.31am	London Bridge		

and as shown Saturdays

Once again long hours on this duty for locomotive and men.

The photographs in this article were taken by Ronald and Bill Allen.

Showing my age again, I suspect most readers will remember listening to 'Two-way family favourites' Sunday lunchtime on the light programme (- if aged under 50 please ignore these first sentences). Each week there was a 'bumper-bundle', so using the same expression we have a definite 'bumper-bundle' of comments appertaining to just one item that appeared in issue No. 16, the underground coach being transported by road from Newport.

I am most grateful to all who have taken the trouble to communicate over this topic, some examples are shown below, not necessarily in any order and with thanks also to all who may have sent what is now duplicate information but is much appreciated all the same. From the interest shown perhaps we should even consider an 'Underground Way'? (Fear not, I jest, and in any event it would not be me doing it. But digressing for a moment, my good friend Dave Smith, formerly the owner of the much lamented Cove Models shop recounts the story of how some years ago when a model of an underground train had just been produced, a customer enquired in all seriousness where such a train might be run.? Sensing there was little opportunity for a sale, Dave made the laconic reply, "Under the floorboards of course".)

But to return to Newport in 1928/29 and with this first from Roger Silsbury, as appeared in the 'Island Railway News' No 47 under the heading 'From the Archives'

"If one discounts the Metropolitan Railway carriages purchased by the Isle of Wight Railway in 1914, most people would say that the first 'proper' Underground vehicles arrived on the Island in 1966, but they would be wrong by some thirty eight years.

"A picture was published in the May 1970 edition of the 'Islander' magazine of an Underground car being hauled by a steam lorry, with a request for information. This original photograph was a general view and Tim Cooper was able to determine that it was taken at the top of Hunny-Hill, Newport and that the lorry was new to Westmores in 1928; the carriage was believed to be one of two built by Leeds Forge in 1914 for the Bakerloo line.

"Further information has now come to light. It is confirmed that the car is a Leeds Forge trailer; the two were 238 (delivered 9/6/14) and 239 (delivered 4/8/14) and renumbered 1698 (6/10/26) and 1699 (14/8/26) respectively. Both were withdrawn on 21/6/28 and disposal from the LER is given as 27/7/28 (1698) and 27/6/28 (1699), although no further details were recorded. Although a number is visible on the print, it is impossible to be certain which one it is. The recent Volume 3 of extracts from the *Isle of Wight County Press* included an item under 1928 relating to a Tube Coach and the complete report, under news for Newport in the edition dated 4th August 1928 reads: "LONDON TUBE COACH IN HIGH STREET. Much interest, not to say apprehension, was caused in the High-street on Thursday morning by the passage from the Quay on its way to Hamstead, near Yarmouth, of an old Piccadilly Tube coach, weighing about 10 tons, which is to be used as a bungalow. The difficult task of conveying it to Hamstead was undertaken by Westmores, Ltd. It was placed on a Sentinel steam-lorry, with a timber carriage behind. Owing to its length considerable difficulty was experienced in negotiating the bend out of Quay-streets into the High-street, and in turning the corner into Lower St. James's-street, but the job was eventually accomplished after some interruption to other traffic."

Tim Cooper and I had scoured the Hamstead area during the early 1970's as a likely area in which to find grounded carriage bodies, but we never found anything remotely resembling an old tube car. Does any reader have any inkling of where the car ended up and its subsequent fate?"

Then on the same subject Keith Gunner who had kindly sought the advice of Brian Hardy of 'Underground News'. Brian comments, "This is one of two trailers built in 1914 by Leeds Forge for the Bakerloo. They were num-

Nothing whatsoever to do with underground vehicles, and instead some old-fashioned logic from our regular scribe and much appreciated supporter, Viv Orchard. The image left arrived recently with an obvious comment. "In the old days thanks to the Railway Clearing House, all buffers and couplings were standardised. As this picture shows, a failed 2BIL EMU could be propelled out of the way at Farnham by a U class steam engine. Today a failed Southern EMU can not be propelled by a South West Trains EMU. Even if there was a locomotive in the area it could not assist as the EMU's have no buffers! Progress? What progress!

bered 238 and 239 and became 1698 and 1699 respectively. They were both withdrawn on 21/6/1928. 1698 was disposed of on 27/7/1928 and 1699 on 27/6/1928. Which one it was I don't know I'm afraid. I can only assume it was going to be used in someone's back yard as an outhouse or the like, as many of the old cars were, especially C&SLR. Certainly I have seen a similar photo of this car before, a long time ago on the IoW, but this photo is a different one.

"One thing is most certain – it is definitely not W&C." Your photograph may have been the proverbial sprat ... as a quick check of original W&C stock details would have shown it clearly not from that source. Hope this will be of interest. Kind regards Keith Gunner - with many thanks to Brian Hardy."

Now from Eric Nicholas, "The picture of the tube car on page 89 of Southern Way 16, is almost certainly a 1914/15 built trailer car for London Electric Railways' use on the Bakerloo Line. The car was probably built by Leeds Forge. This stock was the first to feature a centre door, which was remotely electrically locked by the Gateman. Originally the centre doorway was dual leafed, but these were quickly changed to single leafs, as the double doors were too narrow for passengers to get through. These cars operated on the newly open extension from Paddington to Queens Park, and only operated the Elephant & Castle to Queens Park "Local" service, from the introduction of through Watford Junction trains in 1917. This was the last

tube stock built with end gates. The stock was replaced by 1928 "Standard" stock built by the Union Construction Company, so the car seen here in 1929 has, almost certainly, been sold for scrap."

Then from Peter Swift, "Hello Kevin, The tube car illustrated on page 89 of Southern Way No. 16 is not a Waterloo & City car. The original Waterloo & City cars were not taken out of service until 1940. It is a London Underground car and appears to be one of two trailer cars built in 1914 by Leeds Forge for extensions to the Bakerloo line. Although only 14 years old in 1928, these two cars were non standard and the photograph shows that it retains its open gated end platforms, so was not modernised to run with the "standard" tube stock, which came into service between 1923 and 1934. As it was a trailer car, the only electrical equipment would be the lighting and through control cables."

Finally on this topic from Mark Brinton who has also kindly forwarded the illustration below. Mark comments, "I noted with interest the picture of the underground coach and the Sentinel steam lorry. In my collection I have a picture of what is presumably the same carriage with the same lorry but at a different location. My picture is taken at the top of Hunnyhill (going out of Newport towards Cowes). It is possible that it was taken during the refreshment stop mentioned in your text, as in my photo, the crew are appearing to give some attention to the vehicle. I may be able to shed some light on what the carriage was.

Having shown the picture to some LUL associates a few years ago, they suggested that it was probably an ex. Bakerloo Trailer built by Leeds Forge in 1914. These were withdrawn in 1929-1930.Exactly what it was doing on the Island still remains a bit of a mystery.

"After the end of the First World War and into the 1930s a number of "villages" were established on the Island in locations such as Gurnard, Thorness, Atherfield and Cranmore. These were "constructed" using a significant amount of old railway carriage bodies in addition to old bus and tram bodies, large huts and other similar portable structures. On the Island old railway carriage bodies were in plentiful supply at this time, as the IWR disposed of much of their surplus 4w stock after the war and this was followed in the 1920s and 1930s by various SR stock replacement programmes which generated numerous "scrap" railway carriages suitable for use as holiday homes and summer houses. However, it is known that a number of railway carriage bodies were imported specially for use as holiday homes, there were for instance, three LBSCR carriages of a type not used on the Island incorporated into a house in Freshwater.

"So, if there was a plentiful supply of local carriage bodies, why import? Well looking at Island stock withdrawn in 1929, it consisted of nine ex IWR/Met 8w carriages, most of which ended up as beach huts at St.Helens. In 1930 there were only 2x FYN 4w carriages disposed of. This may have led to a local shortage of carriage bodies and demand being such, that it had to be satisfied by importing from the Mainland. In 1931 local carriage bodies became plentiful again as the SR commenced a programme of replacing the 4w stock (mostly LCDR vehicles by this time) with bogie vehicles. All the above would tend to confirm the date as being 1929-1930 (possibly early 1931), but where was the Underground coach going? Well firstly I am not aware of its existence ever being recorded in any of the "surveys" of IOW Carriage Bodies. However, that may not be surprising as some of the carriage body conversions are hard to spot! Especially, as you would probably be looking for characteristics of a more "traditional" railway carriage. "New" carriage body discoveries do still occur occasionally, so it is possible that this vehicle may still exist, just heavily disguised. The biggest clue we have as to where it was going, has been provided in your caption. Prior to reading this I would have thought that the carriage would have most likely to have been going to Gurnard or Thorness (both near Cowes). However, mention of turning off into Forrest Road, makes this less likely, unless they were going round the back way, which would have been unlikely as these roads are narrow. Forrest Road is the main road from Newport towards Yarmouth and after passing through Shalfleet and Ningwood, the road skirts the edge of the Cranmore "development", so the carriage could have been going there. Incidentally, carriage bodies also were known to be ex-ported from the Island. One NLR First imported to the Island in the 1880s was returned to the Mainland c.1918 and became a grounded body on Hayling Island. It was later returned in the 1970s, and having been given a new underframe now forms part of the IWSR Vintage Train fleet."

Changing the subject now and two comments on different articles recently appeared by David Monk-Steel. The first of these from Peter Clark. "I especially appreciated the article in "Southern Way" No. 13 which was the first fresh information I have read about the effects of the floods since the contemporary accounts published in 1953. Not least, enjoyment came from the fact that it was written by David Monk-Steel who was a colleague (and one of my many bosses!) on the Southern Region in the 1970s. I have long since lost touch with him but we enjoyed many a railway chat over a cup of signal box tea.

"I am puzzled, however, by his assertion that two new signal boxes were built for the reopening of the Canterbury Loop in 1953. From 1946 to 1956, I lived in sight of the Canterbury East-Faversham and Canterbury West-Ashford lines a mile or so south west of Canterbury and the favourite spot for trainspotting was sitting on the level crossing gate over the Elham Valley line (a little bit of track survived) at Harbledown Junction, close to where the LCDR crossed the SER. We knew this area generally as 'Whitehall' - the lane was a continuation of Whitehall Road, Canterbury. I remember Canterbury Jct. 'A' box as one of many local railway landmarks but was less aware of Canterbury Jct. 'B' box as it was further along Whitehall Road towards Canterbury West. Writing in "The Railway Observer" in May 1952, Arthur G. Wells (another local enthusiast who was a very good friend of mine from 1960 until his sad death in 1996) stated that "the two signal boxes are still in position, though boarded up, and all signalling of the two junctions has been removed." It is worth repeating another quote from Arthur, after the loop reopened in 1953, that, because of the gradient between Jct. 'B' and Jct. 'A', an up train would not be accepted by Jct. 'B' from Canterbury West until it had been accepted by Jct. 'A' which in turn would not accept it until it had been offered to Chartham crossing (the next block post towards Selling/Faversham and not to be confused with Chartham *station* on the Ashford line). Once the latter had accepted it, all the signalmen concerned could pull off allowing the train to proceed from Canterbury West with a clear road throughout.

"I don't know when Jct. 'B' box was demolished although parts of the brickwork survive today. Jct. 'A' box was still intact in the 1960s and I think it must also have remained open (or been manned from time to time) after the loop again became disused once the Herne Bay-Birchington section reopened. The last train over the Canterbury Loop is reckoned to have been the RCTS Invicta rail tour on Sunday 12 September 1954, but some days I would go trainspotting at Canterbury East. This meant seeing fewer trains than at

'Whitehall', of course, but there was the chance of a ride on a Fairburn 2-6-4T which brought up a mid-afternoon passenger train from Dover Priory. The engine uncoupled and ran forward over Wincheap bridge, crossed to the down line via the London end crossover and ran back through the station before regaining the up line via the Dover end crossover. It then propelled the coaches over Wincheap bridge but, before it could draw them back to the down platform and return to Dover, a train of ferry vans would pass through and I remember seeing this train waiting at Canterbury Jct. 'A', obviously awaiting acceptance by Canterbury East box. Years later (in 1974) I became a signalman at Canterbury East and the then semaphore down distant was still on the gantry at the site of the junction. Although I experienced longer pulls at other boxes, this was the hardest pull I ever came across and David (who was ASM at Faversham) will probably remember having a go himself.

"Even today, a visit to 'Whitehall' still brings back poignant memories. In 1986 the British Railways Board sought parliamentary powers, not only to reinstate the Canterbury Loop but also to build a new connection from Jct. 'A' down to the Canterbury West line towards Chartham, allowing the section of the latter past Harbledown Jct. to be abandoned. This would probably have been quite short and steep owing to the proximity of the A2 Canterbury bypass road but would have enabled trains to run between Faversham and Ramsgate via Canterbury West again and also between Ashford and Dover Priory via Canterbury East. I doubt, however, if this will ever happen. It would be great if some more unpublished photographs of the Canterbury area might appear in "Southern Way" one day." Yours sincerely Peter Clark. *(Peter, thank you, we too would appreciate more from the Canterbury area - any offers anyone....?)*

David Monk-Steel also comments, "Peter did contact me after the article appeared and it was very pleasant to converse with him. Peter was a great advisor to me when I was a rookie assistant station manager, and he was an experienced signalman. The use of the word 'new' in respect of the signalboxes was careless of me, the signalboxes were in fact mothballed, the Canterbury Loop having been officially closed on 21st October 1951 having been unused for many months previously. The line was in fact doubled as part of this re-opening and new and revised signalling was required, but much of the equipment and the cabins too were still in situ."

Now reference David's more recent piece on the 'C' class tenders (issue No. 16): from Neil Knowlden "David Monk-Steel's analysis of the 'C' class tenders answers some of the 'what' questions ..... but why on earth were only a handful of these tenders modified when all those of the 'D' & 'E' classes were changed ? (incidentally, my photo of No. 31724 - complete with snowplough in 1956 - actually shows a 'D' class tender: the handrails are different

- so David can probably cross that one off the list !) There are two other visual differences that David doesn't mention : 1) a number of later-built locos - including 1293, illustrated - had shallower running plate angles like the 'E' class : presumably 1293 has swapped tenders with an earlier loco at some time ; 2) buffers. All 'C' class locos and tenders started out with either tapered or parallel buffers with small heads but towards the end of Southern days they started to get large-headed stepped buffers on the front (at least). A number of 3500 gallon Maunsell Mogul tenders seem to have swapped this type of buffer for S.E.C.R. tapered ones at around the same period so I wonder if there was a deliberate policy of moving larger buffers where there was greatest overhang - though it certainly wasn't a policy of any great urgency. (Can't blame David for omitting the topic of buffers really - it's a real minefield on ex S.E.C.R. locos !) which has appeared elsewhere ..... at first glance it's a typical pick up goods with two vans of L.M.S. origin, two unidentifiable opens and two brake vans .... but why TWO brake vans - and why, so shortly after nationalisation, is only one a native S.R. 25-tonner ? : might I guess that this is part of the brake van equivalent of the Locomotive Exchanges ...... I've never heard of such an exchange but it makes sense and would explain why an L.N.E.R. brake was so far from home. Maybe someone can throw some light on this ?"

Again from David Monk-Steel, "Neil Knowlden raised a number of points which I am afraid I cannot answer. As I explained in my article it was a rough and ready attempt to understand the why and wherefore of the 'C' class tender, and was complied almost entirely with reference to published photographs and to the RCTS book on SE&CR Locomotives by the late D. L. Bradley. The issue of buffers is one I had not tackled and as Neil rightly points out the subject is a minefield. I did attempt to find out a bit more about the tenders by consulting the locomotive records card held in the NRM at York. Sadly these are incomplete to the point of being sparse, but I do have the tender history of a trio of locomotives which suggest to me that the tenders were not routinely kept with any particular locomotive.

'C class tenders were allocated numbers 2870 to 2977 by the SR which omitted locomotive 685 which had been converted to a saddle tank in 1917. Its tender had been attached to A690 until 1931. I have received a very helpful letter from Eric Youlden who has added some more data which I will incorporate into my lists, but I really need to find the rest of the record cards (does anyone know if these still exist, at PRO Kew perhaps?) There is also a great deal more work to do on liveries which also appears to be a minefield, especially in the transition period between the Southern Railway and British Railways periods. The record cards do also indicate some tenders were fitted with solid centre wheels, although most were spoked, so here is another line of research. Who would have thought that a hum-

Loco	Tender	Attached at	date
31280	2884	Ashford	21-12-1928
	2897	Ashford	29-10-1931
	2917	Ashford	1-10-1947
	2939	Ashford	10-7-1953
	2959	Ashford	22-3-1958
31592	2947	Ashford	21-9-1927
	2902	Ashford	9-5-1930
	2914	Ashford	17-3-1934
	2951	Ashford	28-10-1944
	2921	Ashford	5-11-1948
	2961	Ashford	9-5-1952
	2885	Ashford	6-7-1955
	2885	Re-attached at Ashford	18-2-1961
31691	2958	Ashford	3-12-1927
	2894	Ashford	11-1-1930
	2951	Ashford	16-6-1936
	2919	Ashford	14-10-1944
	2886	Ashford	24-4-1953
	2934	Ashford	31-3-1955
	2962	Ashford	10-6-1957
	2940	Ashford	28-5-1959

ble goods class would prove so interesting?!"

Now for a complete change of tack, this time on the Eastleigh Carriage Works images that appear on page 65 (and thereabouts) of No. 16, from Andy Thornton. "My supposition is that the cantrail panels have been welded in relatively small sections - the bodyside panel on the floor beneath the staging does not include the cantrail panel. The welding process would tend to leave an indentation along its length, flat sheets being welded together on a bench would normally be set up slightly high so as to be flat when the weld has cooled and contracted - not possible in this situation. I suggest that a metallic filler is being applied, such material may be a Lead/Tin alloy, in the manner of solder or whitemetal. The heating torch may be using town gas/ compressed air, the filler material having a relatively low melting point and too much heat would cause unwanted panel distortion, plus delaying setting of the filler. Soft soldering in this manner does not require tinted goggles - the work is heated, but the torch would probably be removed before appling the filler. It is possible that a hotter flame such as oxy-acetlyene is being used with care, there is a lot of metal to heat up!"

Editors note: my apologies, the credit applicable to the images for this article should have been, 'THE GIL & JULIA BROOM COLLECTION, BISHOPSTOKE HISTORY SOCIETY'.

Now from Phil Atkins, "During the past few weeks I have discovered an interesting little footnote concerning W G Hooley (- see article in SW No. 13). In 1910, while a draughtsman still at Beyer, Peacock he executed the general arrangement drawing for the pioneer Beyer Garratt, built the previous year, the 0-4-0 + 0-4-0 for Tasmania, now preserved in working order on the Festiniog Railway. Apparently it was the practice in some drawing offices to delegate the GA to a fairly newly qualified young draughtsman. Hooley certainly didn't design it, this honour was almost certainly due to Samuel Jackson, who performed the necessary calculations (which also survive in Manchester) and who steadily rose through the ranks from apprentice at BP in 1900 until his death in 1944 as a Director of the firm."

Last but by no means least an appeal. Do you or do you know anyone who recalls the canteen at Redhill MPD around 1959/60? Bill Jackson would very much like to find out more on the lady who worked there at that time, 'Daisy' (Wendy) Jones. If anyone knows of any contact details for 'Daisy', or can suggest a contact route it would be much appreciated.

Finally Michael Barnard kindly sent this image of Chatham Viaduct following on from our unknown illustration in SW14. Michael kindly points out his image, right, is the viaduct before the reconstruction seen in SW14. The picture is taken looking down Railway Street towards Chatham Town Hall / centre, Chatham Station is 200 yds or so behind the camera. This in fact is a fairly steep hill leading out of Chatham. The new viaduct was opened in 1902 so I would give a date of 1900/1901.The cost of the new viaduct was reported at £7000 against the estimate of £1500!!

GENERATIONS

1966/67: the final transition from steam on the Southern. We tend to recall the steam engine (of course) but so much else was taking place / changing at the same time. Thanks to Keith Lawrence some at least was recorded for posterity.

Above *- Generations at Waterloo. Electric 'COR', No. 3107, 'Standard 5', 'Warship', and West Country No. 34104. Add to this the signals, the smoke blackened appearance, the platform trolleys etc. etc - all now swept away. 15 August 1966.*
Opposite top *- Loaded (part) cartic wagons at Waterloo, 21 January 1967. 1965 registered 'Vauxhalls' abound.*
Opposite bottom *- BR Mk1 vehicles, as empty stock, being drawn back from Waterloo to Clapham Junction by No. 73169. 15 August 1966. (Mike King comments on the blue / grey Mk 1 seen, "The grey BSK is presumably freshly repainted and has the set No. 107 ready for inclusion in this 3-set from June 1967 (put back a month to July 10 because the electrification wasn't quite ready for the intended start of the Summer timetable). This is one of the sets that appeared on paper but might never have been formed up as such. The June 1967 Carriage Working Notices listed all the coaches with their intended set numbers, but few were actually formed as such. Sets 105-109 were all to be traditionally formed of two brake seconds and a composite in the middle - set 107 to comprise BSKs 34627 and 34628 (ex-set 539 in 1964) along with CK 15582 from set 540 - all already electrically heated and from the SE Division. I have repaint dates of the coaches as follows:*
34627 - 5/6/66. 34628 15/3/66 - which seems awfully early for a blue / grey repaint so might be wrongly noted. 15582 - not recorded. The next coach appears to be a corridor first so could well be empty stock off a boat train but I am surprised that it is in Platform 14 - boat train arrivals were normally dealt with in Nos. 11 or 12 so as to have ready access to the cab road.")

Opposite page, top left - The 'Cunarder' but without its train! 'No. 34034 returning home after taking a train to Southampton Docks clearly without a revenue earning duty back. 9 June 1967.

Opposite page, top right - The analogy is going to be like waiting for a bus: this time it is a relief to the 'Cunarder' that is seen and an effort at replicating a headboard (did it really make a difference?). No. 73020 passing Walton on Thames, 21 June 1967,

Opposite page, bottom - No. 34052, formerly 'Lord Dowding' in Oatlands cutting. 10 May 1967.

This page, top - Tuesday 4 July 1967, less than a week before the end of steam. No. 34019 devoid of its 'Bideford' name heads west past the carriage siding at Walton on Thames.

This page, centre - Oatlands signal box, formerly 'Walton Cutting'. It is seen here on 8 April 1967 with the Walton on Thames station master, Keith Ricketts, at the top of the steps. (Keith Lawrence recalls Mr Ricketts was a great help in the area as did all the staff.) Keith Ricketts later moved to be Area Manager Surbiton, assistant station master Waterloo, and it believed finally station master Portsmouth. Oatlands signal box had opened with the quadrupling of the main line in 1894, it survived until 1970.

This page, bottom - '2HAL' No 2617 leading an EMU formation seen crossing from the down main to the up main at Walton on Thames. 9 April 1967. The number '32' implies a Waterloo - Alton line service.

Opposite top - *A light load for No. 80012, two CCT vans leaving Walton as the 7.00 pm parcels to Feltham. 4 July 1967.*

Opposite bottom - *A '3TIS' and '4VEC' combination on trial at Walton on Thames, 21 January 1967. One of the drivers involved in these trials was Phil Blake, although it is not certain if he was involved on this particular occasion.*

This page , top - *The weedkilling train coming off the Addlestone Loop, 3 July 1967. Propelling was a BR Standard Class 4.*

This page, centre - *Next stop Alton? - I think not. No. 34013 (still displaying its 'Okehampton' nameplate) is in the down bay at Basingstoke, formerly used by trains for the Basingstoke and Alton line, 7 October 1966. The working is a Salisbury line stopping service. The engine has also received some attention with white paint, possibly dating back to March 1966 when it was one of those involved with a tour on the Somerset & Dorset. The new MAS signals will be noted, Basingstoke changed from semaphore to colour lights on 20 November 1966.*

This page, bottom - *Visitor to Eastleigh. No. 45222 was probably awaiting a return to its home territory when recorded at Eastleigh on 30 October 1966. 'R.O' records indicate this engine had been used three times by the SR the previous month to power the 8.35 am Waterloo to Weymouth working - presumably also covering the remainder of the diagram. Evidently the LMR had not been in any hurry to repaint the tender!*

Terry Cole's Rolling Stock File No. 17

SR 'THANET STOCK'

At the Grouping the SECR had no mainline corridor stock apart from the Continental boat train stock (seen in Rolling Stock file No 2). The existing LSWR designed Ironclad stock was too wide for many of the Kent lines so Maunsell and Lynes set about designing a narrower 8ft 6in wide version. The 'Thanet stock' as it became known, was fitted with SR bogies and was similar in appearance to the true Maunsell stock which followed, but had British standard gangways and screw couplings instead of the Pullman gangways and buck-eye couplers with which the later stock would be fitted. At 57 ft body length, they were also 2ft shorter than the subsequent Maunsell stock and were classified 'Restriction 1'. Three types of coach were built at Lancing and Eastleigh in 1924/5. They comprised 18 8-compartment 3rds, Nos. 977 – 994 (to diagram 53), 18 5-compartment 3rd brakes, Nos. 3562 – 3579 (to diagram 165) and 41 7-compartment composites, Nos. 5505 – 5545 (to diagram 317). Together they were initially formed as nine eight-coach trains with five loose composites. The Thanet stock was mainly withdrawn as a result of the Kent Coast electrification on 15 June 1959 and many coaches joined a large number of condemned vehicles awaiting disposal stored on the down line between Horsted Keynes and Ardingly. Several vehicles were fitted with corridor adaptors at some times in their existence to enable them to run with Pullman gangwayed stock.

The compartment side of Thanet composite S 5530 S is seen here in the line of withdrawn coaches on the Ardingly branch, 7 August 1960. The cross within a circle was the 'kiss of death' when applied to vehicles at this period. From the mid 1930s this coach had run as a loose vehicle, but joined set No. 472 for the last two years of its life. It was withdrawn in July 1959.

The end detail of these coaches is clearly shown in this view of the corridor side of a Thanet composite also in the line on 7 August 1960. The third class section has a droplight without a door – the first class has room for a full extra window.

A Thanet Brake 3rd in the long line of condemned coaches on 4 June 1960. The very slight tumblehome at the bottom of the sides can appear flat from some angles. The end section of the coaches was virtually identical to the later Maunsell 'Restriction 1' stock although the Thanet ends were flat. To the right is another Thanet composite whilst the third vehicle with its more curved profile appears to be a Maunsell 'Restriction 4' third. To the left is the end of SEC continental coach No. S 1005 S.

[All photos David Wigley]

The SOUTHERN RAILWAY:
from Inception, through to Nationalisation and beyond.

Part 4 - Continuing Investment

Tony Goodyear

(Previous instalments in this series appeared in Issues 6 , 8 & 13.)

In this article I aim to complete the story of the Eastern section suburban electrification and take a detailed look at the introduction of the world's first 4-aspect colour light signalling system. The ultimate fate of the Brighton overhead is recounted as is the extension of electrification on the former LB&SCR lines as part of the changeover to DC traction. On the rolling stock side we look at the conversion of old steam-hauled suburban stock into smart new electric trains for the second phase of the electrification, albeit just old bodies on new underframes, together with stop-gap corridor carriages for main line services prior to the development of the new Maunsell/ Lynes standardised carriage fleet.

Following the belated introduction of electric services from Charing Cross and Cannon Street to Orpington, Bromley North and The Mid-Kent lines on 28 February 1926, using the "temporary" electrification into Cannon Street and the interim signalling arrangements at Charing Cross, further introductions of electric services on the Dartford loop lines depended on the completion and commissioning of the full facilities at Charing Cross and Cannon Street and, to accommodate the vastly increased services, a new signalling system would also need to be introduced. In 1926 in order to install the new track layout and signalling at Cannon Street, the Southern chose to close the station completely from the afternoon of the 5th June until the early hours of the 28th June.

After the start of "temporary" electric services from Charing Cross and Cannon Street, work was concentrated on completing the electrification to Dartford, described as, "via all three routes". The actual sections electrified created a number of routing possibilities: these were: the Greenwich line from North Kent East Junction to Charlton via Deptford, the North Kent line from St Johns to Dartford via Blackheath and Woolwich, the Bexleyheath line from Blackheath Junction and Crayford Creek Junction and the Dartford Loop from Hither Green to Dartford Junction, together with three spur lines: the Erith Loop, the Crayford Spur and the Lee Spur. All essential works on these lines were completed prior to the complete closure of Cannon Street, and some limited electric services were also run from Charing Cross to Dartford during the General Strike, which took place between 10th and 16th May 1926.

Prior to the temporary closure of Cannon Street for remodelling work, a number of enhancements were made elsewhere to accommodate displaced services. Many of the services that normally used Cannon Street were diverted to Charing Cross or terminated short at London Bridge. From

Opposite top – A last look at the "Elevated Electric" probably in the early months of 1928 the conductor rail is down and the new Westinghouse colour light signals are installed ready for introduction on the 17 June 1928. In the bottom right hand corner of the frame the top of one of the two aspect ground signals can just be seen.

Opposite bottom left – Cannon Street before the remodelling and resignalling (taken on Saturday 5th June 1926).

Opposite bottom right – Cannon Street after remodelling and resignalling (taken on Monday 23rd June 1926).

Looking at the two photographs the amount of work carried out in just 18 days is quite remarkable. The extent of the temporary electrification can clearly be seen in the first picture as only the left hand most four tracks have conductor rail installed, even so the final electrification only shows five roads electrified (platforms 1 – 5) at this time, platforms 6, 7 and 8 remaining un-electrified.

Cluster signal head (left) and Vertical signal head (right) as supplied by Westinghouse on their three signalling contracts. The aspects displayed by these signals were as follows: cluster head, right lens = red, bottom lens = first yellow, left lens = green, top lens = second yellow, vertical head, bottom lens = first yellow, second lens = red, third lens = second yellow, top lens = green.

June 6th 1926 these services were converted to electric working and it is likely that at least two of the Eastern Section (low level) terminal platforms at London Bridge were also electrified, to accommodate the additional 23 trains that were booked to terminate at London Bridge during the morning peak. The remaining 58 trains were somehow squeezed in at Charing Cross.

During the just over three weeks closure of Cannon Street station, around 1,000 men were employed on the various tasks involved with installing the new layout and about three quarters of them were working shifts. The first part of the work involved the removal of the existing track layout and old signalling. A fair amount of the temporary electrification equipment would also have been removed and put to one side and subsequently much of it was incorporated into the new layout. While the platforms were rebuilt and the site prepared, the new track layout was taking shape at New Cross Gate, where it was laid out on a piece of flat ground, a common practice in later years. Once laid out and checked the layout would have all the necessary

holes drilled in the rails for the: stretcher bars, electrical track bonding and point machine fittings. The insulated track circuit joints (Insulated Block Joints or IBJs) would also be trial fitted, if possible. When the entire layout had been checked, the individual parts would be numbered and the layout broken down into manageable sections for transport round to Cannon Street. The whole operation, from assembly to final commissioning, was carried out rather like a military campaign. The sections of the new layout were delivered to the work site in a prearranged order, so that all the pieces fitted together like a jigsaw puzzle. Following the installation of the individual point work and the adjoining permanent way, the signalling and electrification engineers would descend to complete their work before everything was tested and signed off ready for use.

Apart from the pure electrification works there were also the added infrastructure elements of remodelling the layouts at the other main stations to improve operating flexibility, and eliminate facilities that were no longer required. To get the best out of these revised facilities new signalling was also provided in the immediate area around the main London city terminals. These signalling systems were a step change away from anything installed in this country before. The first section of new signalling to be introduced was for the lines around Holborn Viaduct and Blackfriars. The changes to the physical layout were described in Part 3 – The Priorities (SW 13). The signalling, loosely based on North American practice, was designed and supplied by Siemens General Electric (SGE) under contract, with most of the installation work being carried out by the Southern Railway's own signalling teams. As a result of using a foreign-based contractor, a high proportion of the equipment supplied came from overseas sources, the signals even having distinctly American-looking finials. This was also the first installation of 4-aspect colour light signalling anywhere in the world. The running signals provided were of two distinct types, vertical and cluster; the former being direct ancestors of the signals we see today, with the aspects arranged vertically with an oblong surround and a separate signal mounted to one side or the other for a diverging move. Additionally the signal heads were mounted forward of the round signal post. The cluster style signals were principally used where space precluded the use of a vertical signal. Additionally large route indicators were provided where multiple routing possibilities existed, miniature two-aspect shunt signals being provided on the ground for shunt moves or bracketed out from the main signal post for facing moves into sidings. The other main difference to current practice was in the positioning of the aspects displayed by the main signals, which was from the top: green, yellow, red, yellow, whereas the current practice is: yellow, green, yellow, red. The new signalling was controlled from a new 120 lever mechanically-locked power frame in a new signal box at Blackfriars Junction and a new 86 lever mechanically-

This atmospheric picture taken at Blackfriars on a typically cold murky day in December 1946, with the road off for the Down Through, what appears to be the driver, is hurrying towards the cab complete with his 'Gladstone Bag'. The two units visible are 3 SUB units with rebuilt ex SE&CR bodies (see text).

locked power frame which was installed in the existing signal box at Holborn Viaduct. The new signalling on this section was introduced on 21st March 1926, replacing seven mechanical boxes.

Just over three months later, on Sunday 27th June 1926 new 4-aspect signalling was introduced between Charing Cross – Metropolitan Junction – Cannon Street & Borough Market Junction. The new signalling interfaced with the recently introduced signalling between Blackfriars Junction and Metropolitan Junction on the Ludgate Spur lines, the eastern end being controlled by Metropolitan Junction together with the entry and exit to nearby Ewer Street locomotive stabling point. Interim electric services to Dartford began the following day. In this case the contract for the signalling system was let to the Westinghouse Brake & Signal Company (WB&SCo.) in October 1925 and was the first of three major signalling contracts for the company in connection with the re-signalling works on the Eastern and Central sections. Although similar in concept to the

SGE installation at Blackfriars, the equipment supplied was very different in design. A new signal box was provided at Charing Cross, on the overhead gantry at the eastern end of the platforms (see picture SW 13 p 94), which received a 107 lever Westinghouse-style 'K' miniature lever frame. The second new signal box was provided at Cannon Street and was constructed of timber on the western side of the bridge, close to the station. It too was fitted with a Westinghouse 'K' frame, this time a 143 lever version. At Metropolitan Junction the existing signal box was retained, together with a 60 lever, Evans O'Donnell mechanical frame (there is some confusion as to whether this frame was the original or a replacement but as the old frame is listed as having 100 levers, it was probably a replacement). In any event the frame was upgraded to control the new layout, originally only the main running signals being electrically operated, with the points and ground signals being worked mechanically. Six old mechanical signal boxes were abolished as a result of the introduction of the new

The new 107 lever K style as installed at Charing Cross and brought into use on 27th June 1926. An external view of the new signal box is shown on page 98 of SW 13. Compare this K style lever frame with the view of new North Kent East L style frame on page 96 and the differences start to become apparent: glass fronted covers for the electric locking, lever labels carried on a cantilevered extension fitted to the front of the frame, the levers on the L frame are also noticeably shorter, to name but a few.

Grove Park 28th February 1926, the first day of electric services to Orpington, Bromley North and the Mid Kent Line. As mentioned in Part 3 the introduction of these services was delayed by three months, the original date being 1st December 1925 but yet again the power supplies were not ready.

signalling, the number of levers in each box being shown in brackets: Charing Cross (130), Cannon Street No.1 (245), Cannon Street No.2 (97), Belvedere Road (100), Waterloo Junction Station (45) and Union Street (20).

The New Westinghouse-style 'K' power frames (not to be confused with the later and more well known style 'L' frames, both types being generally referred to as "miniature lever frames"), were mechanically interlocked, the tappets being driven off the lever at the front of the frame. The electrical circuits were at the back and rear of the frame and rotated via a bevel gear. The main visible distinguishing features though, were the wooden teak casing (with removable glazed access covers), and the lever plates also had slightly rounded corners. The majority of the signals provided were of the vertical type, but with a wider surround than the SGE ones and rounded at the top and bottom. The signal head casting was mounted directly on to the round signal post and secured with bolts tapped through

the casting, with the cables being run up through the centre of the post (as a result, if not properly sealed, all kinds of invertebrate life forms could found living inside when the door at the back was opened). Two-aspect ground level shunt signals were provided, and as before were mounted on a main signal post when required.

For these early colour light signalling schemes the power was derived from the London Electric Supply Company's supply to the combined sub-station and switching centre at Lewisham. In addition to the four main 1,500kW rotary converters supplying the third rail, there were also three 400kW frequency converters which produced a single phase 3.3kV supply at 75 cycles (Hz), for services. This supply was eventually distributed throughout the London area, supplying lighting to some stations and offices but was particularly used for supplying signalling, signal boxes and controller rooms, where it was transformed to 415v or 110v for local distribution to lineside functions,

such as track circuits and signals. For the point machines, a 130v DC supply was required. This was achieved by trickle charging a large lead acid battery (the development of powerful rectifiers capable of supporting the starting current of several point machines at once was still some way in the future). The use of 75 Hz frequency was not thought of as a problem at the time, particularly as this was in common use in the London area, but following the creation of the National Grid a standard national frequency of 50 Hz was settled on. While the change was of little consequence to domestic users, to the railways and other commercial customers that had machinery designed to work on other frequencies the change was an expensive exercise. Having its own frequency converters and dedicated supply network the railway did no more than maintain the status quo, only changing equipment to 50Hz operation as and when major re-signalling schemes or rebuilding works were carried out, some 75Hz equipment even surviving in use well into the 1980s.

Soon after the completion of the signalling improvements between the city terminals and London Bridge, it was announced, on 9th August 1926, that the Brighton Line AC overhead electrification system would be replaced by third rail DC electrification. Not only was all the existing overhead electrification to be converted to DC but a number of additional lines were to be electrified at the same time. These additional sections were: London Bridge Main Lines (and Spur Lines from South Bermondsey Junction) to Norwood Junction, Sydenham Junction to Crystal Palace (Low Level), Bromley Junction to Beckenham Junction, Herne Hill to Tulse Hill, Streatham to Epsom, Streatham South Junction to Wimbledon and Sutton to Epsom Downs. In fact the section from Streatham as far as Cheam via Mitcham Junction formed part of the LB&SCR's original Sutton extension proposals back in 1913, but was never completed.

In November 1927 it was announced that as part of the associated works colour light signalling would be further extended from Borough Market Junction through London Bridge to Spa Road, Bricklayers Arms and Old Kent Road Junction. An order for the supply of signalling equipment and other works was given to WB&SCo. in October 1927. The improvement works included a major rearrangement of the Central section tracks between London Bridge – Bricklayers Arms Junction and Old Kent Road on the South London lines. The old arrangement of the South London

tracks starting on the South side, was Up South London Line, Reversible Line, Down South London Line, at South Bermondsey Junction the three lines split, those to Bricklayers Arms Junction continuing on their own viaduct in the same configuration, and those to Peckham Rye becoming one Down Line and two Up Lines between South Bermondsey Junction and Peckham Rye. On the South London Lines, between London Bridge and South Bermondsey Junction, there were two intermediate signal boxes at St James' Road and Abbey Street. The other three lines were worked from Eastern section boxes at Spa Road and Blue Anchor. All six lines were rearranged to become, Up South London (no change) Down South London (previously Reversible Line), Up Local (previously Down South London Line), Up Through (previously Up Line), Down Through (previously Down Line) and Down Local (previously also shown as a Down Line). Following the rearrangement, only the Up and Down South London Lines had a physical junction with the line to Peckham Rye, and this would have resulted in South Bermondsey Station only having up platforms. Consequently it was decided to relocate the station a few hundred yards beyond the junction on the Peckham Rye line. The new station was in the usual form of a 520ft island platform, but this time the surface was of timber (probably to reduce weight) as it was constructed on arches with stairs through one arch leading to the booking office by the main road. To create the space for the new station the middle track (a second up line) was taken out of use before the start of the main engineering works on 7th/8th January 1928, and the track was lifted between South Bermondsey Junction and Old Kent Road Junction.

On the 25th March 1928 the first 3rd rail DC electric trains started running on the Central Section and initially they were confined to the newly-electrified main lines via New Cross Gate. These services were a direct replacement for the previous steam trains and ran in the existing timings. The services concerned ran from Charing Cross, Cannon Street or London Bridge to: Caterham, Tattenham Corner and Crystal Palace (Low Level) via Sydenham Junction. Before the main changeover from AC to DC traction could take place, the new signalling needed to be installed and commissioned, to accommodate the changed running on the South London Lines. WB&SCo. supplied two new style 'K' miniature lever frames. The first, with just 35 levers, was installed in the existing signal box at Borough Market Junction. The second frame for London

Opposite top – London Bridge new signal box with construction work almost complete, the windows of the second story (housing the mechanical locking) were bricked up during the war. This view is taken from behind the turntable, which was situated in the wide way that existed between the South London Lines and the LB&SCR Main Lines on the approach to the platforms.

Opposite bottom – A view showing almost the complete London Bridge frame of 311 levers, together with the operating floor and the two illuminated diagrams. The South London platforms had the lowest numbered levers (highest numbered platforms), the highest numbered levers were on the No. 1 & 2 Down Lines (the two northernmost tracks ultimately lead to the Down Greenwich Line at North Kent East Junction).

Bridge was on an altogether different scale, having 311 levers (some authors state 312 but Westinghouse's own publicity material states 311, and I think they should know). A new three-storey purpose-built signal box was provided and was situated just beyond the dividing wall, which supported the overall roof, between the Brighton side and the Low level (South Eastern platforms). The new building was most substantial and constructed of steel-framed brick and measured 113ft. long by 14ft 7ins. wide. There were three floors. The ground floor contained the Relay Room which housed all the relays for track circuit, detection, line and repeater functions for the local area up to approx. 500 yds., together with the fuse and terminal boards. Built on the same (ground) level, in the form of an annex were the power and battery rooms, mess rooms and workshops. The first (middle) floor provided access to the majority of the mechanical locking, which extended down from the second (top) floor. The second floor itself contains the 311 lever 'K' style power frame, together with two "spot light type" illuminated diagrams and all the other operating equipment ranging from block bells, train describers to telephones and booking boys' desks. London Bridge has another claim to fame, as it had the highest number of levers in a single mechanically-locked lever frame in the country. On completion of the signalling works the following ten existing signal boxes were abolished (number of levers in brackets) Borough Market Junction (21), London Bridge A (41), B (148) C (47), N (280), S (98), Abbey Street (22), St. James' Road (23), Up Croydon Line (12) and South Bermondsey Junction (56).

The introduction of both the new signalling and DC electrification on the South London lines took place on the 17th June 1928, following completion of the remaining preparatory work, the largest item of which was the partial reconstruction of Tulse Hill station and the bridge over Norwood Road at the South end of the station which was also reconstructed to provide parallel running to West Norwood and Streatham or Streatham Hill. All AC overhead electric services radiating from London Bridge were discontinued at the same time. For the first few weeks of the new services some trains were terminated short at Crystal Palace or diverted into Victoria. These diversions also included some of the remaining steam services. The new services that were introduced on and from 18th June 1928 exploited a number of new roundabout service opportunities so characteristic of Southern operations. The London Bridge to Crystal Palace (Low Level) via Sydenham service, which was introduced on the 25th March, was extended through to London Bridge via Tulse Hill. The other roundabout service circulated from London Bridge and back via Norwood Junction, Selhurst and Streatham. New out and back services to Epsom Downs (fast to Norwood Junction) and Coulsdon North (fast to Norwood Junction) via the main line were also introduced; out and

back services via the South London Line to Streatham Hill and Victoria were direct replacements for services previously operated by the overhead electrics. The South London services were very much reduced in frequency from those previously offered, the service having never regained the patronage lost when it suffered a four month closure during the 1926 miner's strike. In connection with the diversion of trains from the Croydon lines that terminated at Charing Cross or Cannon Street into London Bridge during the peak hours, a letter was sent to season-ticket holders explaining the reason for the changes, no doubt penned by John Elliott but signed by Sir Herbert Walker. The text of that letter is reproduced below:

"As already announced, new electric services will be inaugurated on Sunday, June 17 next, between London Bridge and numerous stations in the Central Section suburban area. For some time past it has been a matter of increasing difficulty to run the morning and evening business trains from the Croydon lines to and from Charing Cross and Cannon Street stations, owing to the fact that such trains have to cross the tracks south of London Bridge High Level station, of trains from other areas.

"With the introduction of electric working in March last on the Caterham and Tadworth branches it was necessary to terminate business trains from these lines at London Bridge station, and with the greatly increased number of electric trains which will be running on the Croydon lines on and from June 17 next, it will be necessary to apply the same arrangement to the business trains from Gomshall, Reigate, Redhill, Nutfield, Merstham, &c.

"These trains will therefore run to and from London Bridge station in the business hours, but in the non-business hours and on Sundays services will continue to be given beyond London Bridge station. In order to facilitate the exchange of passengers desiring to travel to and from Charing Cross and Cannon Street stations by rail, the overbridge has been extended from the High Level to the Low level stations, and an opening has been provided from the Central Section station

"The decision to terminate the business trains at London Bridge has, it is hardly necessary to state, been arrived at only after the most careful consideration by the directors, and has been dictated by the ever-increasing traffic on our suburban lines. Various ways of dealing with this traffic have been thoroughly examined, and the principle of allocating definite terminal stations for trains from each area (thereby facilitating and improving the working) will, I am confident, give the best results in the interests of our passengers as a whole."

The second and final phase in the abolition of the 'Elevated Electric' took place just about nine months later on 3rd March 1929, when DC services replaced the AC services

North Kent East Junction showing the old and the new signal boxes on the same overline structure, the small building in the foreground is the battery room and linesman's hut. On the overline gantry in the distance can be seen one of the other six old signal boxes (most likely Surrey Canal Junction) that were replaced as part of the provision of colour light signalling. One of the new signal gantries can also be seen through the structure on the right before the old signal gantry.

from Victoria (see SW 13 for details). Additionally some services were extended and some new possibilities exploited. The most notable of these were new services from both London Bridge and Victoria via Mitcham Junction (not previously electrified) to Epsom, the London Bridge trains carrying on over the Western section electrified tracks from Waterloo to Effingham Junction or Dorking North. It should also be noted that the 3¾ mile section between the old L&SWR station at Epsom and Leatherhead was previously (before the grouping) a L&SWR/LB&SCR joint line, both companies having their own stations in Epsom and Leatherhead, an extravagance soon rectified by the new Southern management team. Leatherhead's L&SWR station was the first to go on 10th July 1927, all trains thereafter using the former LB&SCR station, and then via a new link at the South end of the station to rejoin the Effingham line. Surprisingly the old station site was used right up to the 1970s for stabling

electric stock, and the embankment retaining wall is still passed when using town's gyratory road system. Epsom, on the other hand, received a brand new station (currently the subject of development proposals) adjacent to the town centre, on the site previously occupied by the old L&SWR station. The station was opened on 3rd March 1929 to coincide with the introduction of electric services to London Bridge and Victoria, as well as accommodating the existing electric services to Waterloo, previously introduced on 12th July 1925. The LB&SCR's Epsom Town station also closed on the 3rd March 1929, but in this case it survived as the town's goods depot until the mid 1960s, by which time it had been reduced to a coal depot, and was closed together with the signal box when the traffic was transferred to the new Tolworth Coal Concentration Depot.

Another new service ran from Holborn Viaduct to Wimbledon via Tulse Hill and Haydons Road. In fact, the line continued on back to Tooting via Merton Park and

The first Westinghouse style L all electric 87 lever frame installed in the new North Kent East Junction signal box, built alongside the old mechanical one.

Merton Abbey rejoining the original route at Tooting Junction. The section between Merton Park and Tooting was closed to passenger traffic on the introduction of the Wimbledon electric service. The line was retained for freight traffic, right through to Tooting. The large yard at Tooting was beside the Streatham Junction- Wimbledon line, but in later years at least was only accessed from the branch, the freight service surviving to 5th May 1975. The existing service from Victoria to Crystal Palace (Low Level) was changed to DC working and extended through to Beckenham Junction, following considerable expense to upgrade the line between Bromley Junction and Beckenham Junction to accommodate regular traffic, which included the provision of separate running lines alongside the Chatham main lines as far as Beckenham Junction, together with the provision of a new signal box. A new station was also provided at Birkbeck opening a year later on the 2nd March 1930 (now also a tram stop on the London (Croydon) Tramlink). To provide power for the newly-electrified areas on the Central section, the existing Lewisham Electrical Control room was extended. New cables were run to

substations, each having two or three 1,500kW rotary converters, situated at: Tulse Hill, Streatham, Sutton, Forest Hill, Norwood, Purley, Kingswood and Warlingham. The existing Clapham Junction substation, supplied from the power house at Durnsford Road, was extended, with additional convertors to provide power locally.

Moving back to events on the Eastern section, SGE's second signalling contract for the Southern Railway was for the supply of the equipment related to the installation of colour light signalling between New Cross and Blackheath, Hither Green and Ladywell. Two new signal boxes at St Johns and Parks Bridge Junction were provided by the Southern Railway, with continuous automatic 4-aspect signals installed between signal boxes. As part of this scheme the Greenwich Park branch (one of the SE&CR's perceived electrification difficulties) was refurbished as far as the old Lewisham Road station where a new viaduct was constructed to carry the line over the main line between St Johns and Parks Bridge Junction, and then on to connect with the Blackheath and Mid Kent lines at Lewisham station. A second new spur was constructed from the Mid-Kent lines to connect with the Up and Down Main Local lines about ½ a mile before Hither Green station. This line was known as the Lewisham or Courthill Loop.

A third signalling contract was let, to WB&SCo. in January 1929, for signalling works and equipment in connection with the DC electrification on the Eastern and Central sections. This contract was intended to eliminate the remaining semaphore signalling on the Eastern section between the end of the recent London Bridge works and the existing section of automatic signalling between New Cross and St. Johns on the Main Lines and Greenwich on the Greenwich Lines. Six mechanical signal boxes were required to control the short (1¼ miles) section of line between Spa Road and New Cross, all of which were constructed on arches. Some difficulty was experienced when it came to finding a suitable site for the new signal box, often a problem in the London area. In this case the solution was to reuse the old elevated structure on which the old North Kent East box was built, the new box being built in front of the old one, which in turn was removed shortly after the new box was commissioned. The Westinghouse 'K' type lever frames with their mechanical locking were particularly heavy. Fortunately Westinghouse were able to offer a new type of all electric power frame, the style 'L', where the elimination of heavy mechanical locking produced a significant weight saving and hence a new 83 lever style 'L' frame was installed in the new signal box. North Kent East was therefore the first 'L' frame, predating Brighton by nearly 3 years, there were other improvements too: direct operation of points up to ¾ of a mile away and the use of space-saving metal rectifiers (at least that's what's claimed in WB&SCo's. publicity material). The linesman's quarters and battery room were at ground level but the relay room was adjacent to the signalling floor, on the upper deck. Mainly 4-aspect signals were provided with just a few 3-aspect signals on the approaches and the Bricklayers arms goods branch, the remaining Up Line mechanical signals on the Greenwich line had their distant arms replaced by three aspect approach lights. The new signalling was introduced on 1st December 1929 and the following signal boxes were abolished (number of levers in brackets): Spa Road (52), Blue Anchor (22), Southwark Park Junction (44), Surrey Canal Junction (72), North Kent East Junction (70) and New Cross A (79).

Before leaving the subject of signalling it is worth looking at the magnitude of the task that was undertaken. There appear to have been five separate signalling contracts, two placed with Siemens-General Electric and three with WB&SCo. From the award of the first contract to SGE sometime during the middle of 1925, through to the completion of the re-signalling works covering the North Kent East Junction area on 1st December 1929, it had taken a total of about four and a half years to complete the programme of re-signalling works. Many of the key introductions were also arranged to coincide with the introduction of new or changed electrification, or changes to the infrastructure. The other point to note is that each of the five separate contracts was a complete and viable piece of work in its own right. It was not therefore, dependent on the completion of a future contract before the operating benefits and a return on the investment were obtained.

As part of Eastern section electrification scheme a new train maintenance depot was established at Slade Green. Cleaning and inspection sheds were constructed at Orpington and Addiscombe. With similar functions to the one at Effingham Junction, both were opened in time for the introduction of services from Victoria and Holborn Viaduct (see Part 3, SW13). The depot at Slade Green was on an altogether grander scale. It was also unusual in that the Inspection shed was converted from the old locomotive running shed, being 598 ft. long by 117ft. wide with eight roads, and as such it was ideal for the job. Two turntables had been provided in the yard as part of the old layout, one at each end of the through shed; both were removed as part of the conversion. The one at the Dartford (South) end went very early on in the process, to provide space for the new repair shop access roads. The work on converting the shed for its new role was started in late 1925 and was carried out in stages, while still remaining an operational steam shed and it is recorded that the newly-laid conductor rails were at times buried in ash. Towards the end of steam operation the shed was used by both steam and electric trains, with about half being used by the new electric trains and the rest for the servicing the rapidly diminishing steam fleet. This was reduced from 100 to about 55 working engines by the end. It also appears that most of the remaining locos were gone within a couple of weeks of the changeover, either reallocated or sent for scrapping with just a few locos, presumably those unfit to travel, broken up on site. The repair shop was constructed on a new site at the Dartford end of the depot, the land being purchased by the Southern railway in April 1925. The site was quickly cleared and construction of the 500ft. long by 123ft. wide six-road building was largely complete by the end of the year.

It is clear from the above that many more electric units would be required in addition to the 29 new units obtained for the initial service requirements on the Eastern section. The additional units were true rebuilds along the lines of the original L&SWR units but these were more comprehensive reincarnation. The units were effectively old bodies on new underframes, but needless to say it was somewhat more involved than that, as the rebuilt vehicles were provided with a new standard SR 61ft. 11in. underframe, with a 62ft. body built on top formed mostly from the bodies of former 4- & 6-wheel stock, the old chassis being scrapped. Additional sections were spliced in as required. The new underframes were constructed at Lancing, with Ashford assisting by manufacturing some parts and also carrying out pre-assembly work, particularly during the early years of the conversion programme. Ashford was also responsible for bodywork reconstruction, with Eastleigh taking on small batches when the need arose.

Although being rundown as a carriage works, Brighton continued carrying out finishing work, such as upholstery and painting, until this too was phased out and all remaining work was transferred to Lancing.

The first batch of 3-SUB units for the Eastern section, were rebuilt using the bodywork from former SE&CR stock, often of comparatively recent construction. If the allocated number sequence is anything to go by, the first ninety five units 1401-95 were ordered before the twenty-eight contractor-built sets, which carried Nos. 1496-1524, for the initial services from Victoria and Holborn Viaduct. A further ten units to the SE&CR design were added later; they were numbered 1525-34. It is almost certainly the early withdrawal of the steam stock used to create these two batches of electric trains that was so much criticised in the London press. The formation of all these early SE&CR and the first few ex-LB&SCR conversions was Driving Motor Brake Third (DMBT), Trailer Composite (TC) and Driving Motor Brake Composite (DMBC). Deliveries commenced during 1925 although the units were initially slow to appear; but by 1926 rebuilt sets were being delivered at a rate of one or two per week. In order to augment these sets to 8-car formation during the rush-hour services 67 (or 70 depending on the information source) 2-car trailer sets numbered 1051-1117 or 1120 were formed using ex LB&SCR nine-compartment. vehicles (note. the odd three sets may have been formed later). Generally the trailer sets were not subject to the major rebuilding that was given to the electric sets but they did receive what amounted to a comprehensive overhaul. The next batch of thirty 3-SUB units, again with SE&CR bodywork appeared in 1927/8 and were numbered 1601-1630, however they differed from the earlier units in having electrical equipment supplied by Metrovick and appear to have been the first units to employ the Southern's central buffer and rubbing plate couplings within the unit, rather than the MCB automatic couplers used on the contractor-built units and the first two batches of rebuilt stock. The use of the automatic couplers was discontinued following a number of incidents of trains splitting while in service, causing significant delays.

As the electrification programme proceeded on the Eastern and Central sections, yet more units were required, and with almost all of the immediately available former SE&CR steam stock already converted into electric stock a start was made on rebuilding the remaining former LB&SCR seven-coach, steam, bogie block sets. Many of these coaches had been converted into the trailer sets (mentioned above), earlier in the programme. Now the remainder, together with some of the recently withdrawn overhead electric stock, were rebuilt into DC electric units. The first batch of 15 units was built in 1928, numbered 1702-16 and was very similar in layout to the SE&CR sets, being made up of a DMBT, TC and a DMBC. The next batch of

27 units, numbered 1631-57 was created in 1928/9 and differed in their make up by having two DMBT's, and were formed thus: DMBT, TC, DMBT, this reduced the first class accommodation by 24 seats but had an additional 40 third class seats. These sets were also six tons lighter, at 104 tons, than the heaver SE&CR sets at 110 tons. A further five similar sets; numbered 1797-1801 were added in 1931/2. A final batch of 3-SUB units for the 1928/9 electrification numbered 1717-72 reverted to the original DMBT, TC, and DMBC formation. Almost all of the vehicles used in these sets were converted from the remaining former LB&SCR overhead electric stock, mostly of CP and CW types, but the former SL driving trailers (created when the South London sets were split up) were also rebuilt as part of this batch, with just a few vehicles taken from other stock to make up the numbers. Additional trailer sets numbered 1121-67 were also made up in 1928/9 to accompany the new sets using an ex-L&SWR 11-compartment bogie vehicle and a 48ft. 8-compartment SE&CR bogie coach, taken from a batch of 65 built between 1900 and 1906.

While the Southern's Carriage works at Ashford, Brighton and Lancing were kept busy building new underframes and converting many compartment-type vehicles into electric trains, Eastleigh carriage works was mostly engaged on remedying the shortage of mainline corridor stock single-handed – well, nearly! In fact all the main works were initially engaged on finishing off orders already put in hand by the previous authorities, in most cases these orders were for much needed corridor stock. Brighton works, however, was still building new compartment stock, namely the completion of a batch of ten 54ft 7-compartment Lavatory Composites (although three of the first class compartments did not have access to a lavatory), and a batch of ten 54ft 8-compartment Composites (one of which still survives as No. 6349 on the Isle of Wight).

Under Maunsell the SE&CR had been exercising its collective mind on how best to remedy the appalling lack of modern corridor stock available to the operating department, something for which they were much criticised. The problem was tackled from two angles on the basis that they mainly had three types of traffic, namely: premium first, second and third class boat train traffic, long distance commuting to London from the coastal ports and the larger towns of East Kent, together with some long distance traffic to and from the Midlands and the North of England. To cater for the latter traffic the SE&CR had built seven Corridor Composite Brakes (50ft 1in over the body) in 1907 and fitted with British Standard gangways, to cater for the through traffic to other lines. In 1920 the SE&CR built six corridor thirds (54ft 1in over the body, 8ft 6in wide), to a completely new design by the Maunsell/Lynes team. With just six carriages in the batch they must have been seen as some sort of prototypes. They were fitted with British

Standard gangways and screw couplings, the commode handles and door ventilators being very SE&CR. Most of them ran with the corridor composites for some years, both singularly and as the centre car of *ad hoc* three-car sets. Very early in its existence the Southern ordered a further 72 similar vehicles, in the form of nine eight-coach trains nominally consisting of: a brake second at each end, two thirds and four composites. Additionally there were a further five loose composites. All these vehicles were 57ft over the body and 8ft 6in wide (restriction 1) and all became collectively known as 'Thanets' or more correctly 'Thanet stock'.

On the other hand at the grouping Ashford works were just finishing off the second batch of 16 Continentals. These vehicles were similar to the first batch of eight completed in 1921. In theory at least, they were formed into eight-car sets (510/11/12) but seldom appeared as such, a Pullman car often being added and the sets being adjusted in seating capacity to suit the time of year and the working. Any spare cars were then used on other boat train services, when required. These vehicles were the first Southern carriages to have Pullman gangways and buckeye couplings, albeit in this case only within the set, as the brake vehicles only had a gangway connection at the accommodation end, the van end having standard screw couplings. The first 24 vehicles were all built to the narrow width of 8ft 0¾in later known as restriction '0' and as such they could even work over the Hastings Line, and did so in later years. The demand for additional quality stock, for the increasing boat train traffic, was so great that in October 1923 the Southern Railway placed contracts with outside contractors for a further 41 vehicles for early delivery, all being placed in traffic by October 1924. The order was split between Birmingham Railway Carriage & Wagon Co. (BRC&W) (32 vehicles) and Metropolitan Carriage, Wagon & Finance Co. (MCW&F) (9 vehicles). This and a further batch of ten vehicles built at Eastleigh, probably on underframes supplied by MCW&F and delivered in 1927, were built to the slightly wider 8ft 6½ in restriction '1' width. Their main distinguishing feature though, and the one for which they will always be remembered, was their continental style inward opening passenger doors, which gave rise to their universal nick name of 'Continentals'.

Although the L&SWR had passed on to the Southern Railway over 300 corridor carriages at the grouping, under Surrey Warner they were also developing a new range of steel-sheeted flush-sided carriages. The first of these carriages was authorised in 1915 but did not appear until 1921, in the form of four five-carriage trains for the Bournemouth line. They were similar to the latest 'Thanets' from the SE&CR, described above, in being 57ft long, fitted with screw couplings and British Standard gangways but at 9ft wide, they were more substantial vehicles. The early vehicles of this type were also given massive 9ft double-

framed bogies which only added to the overall impression of bulkiness, giving rise to their universal nickname of 'Ironclads'. The sets were formed: four-compartment. Brake Third, eight compartment Third, seven compartment First, seven compartment Pantry Third (really an eight compartment third with one compartment and the toilet space fitted-out as a pantry), four compartment Brake Third. The L&SWR had placed orders for further vehicles of this type in 1917: 2 First and Second class 10-carriage sets plus luggage vans for boat train traffic. They appeared in 1922 formed of eight corridor Firsts sandwiched between 2 Pantry Brake Firsts, and further orders were placed in May 1921, this time for four more five-carriage sets for the Bournemouth line, with two Standard Thirds rather than a Pantry Third in each set, together with 24 loose carriages and two Dining Saloons. Subsequently two further five-car sets were ordered for the Portsmouth line. All the sets were delivered towards the end of 1923, made up of five cars.

The Portsmouth line sets were made up to six coaches by the inclusion of a Dining Saloon. The Dining Saloons arrived at about the same time, and the rest of the loose stock followed in early in 1924, which completed all the outstanding orders placed by the L&SWR. As on the South Eastern, the Southern's desperate need for more corridor stock overrode the desire to introduce the new standard design being developed under Maunsell's guidance by Lynes. Hence further 'Ironclads' were ordered early in 1924. In this case the order consisted of four five-coach sets for Waterloo-Bournemouth traffic and five two-coach sets mainly for the Waterloo-Lymington and Waterloo-Swanage through services. Two final orders were placed for 'Ironclads' but this time for Central section services in the form of two eleven-coach sets for London-Brighton and London-Worthing and Bognor services. Even so, the two sets were somewhat different in their formations and, in their original form, were not interchangeable on their respective duties. The first set for Brighton line services was built at Lancing, the only 'Ironclads' not built at Eastleigh, but also the last entirely new vehicles built at Lancing, being completed in December 1925. The second set, intended for Worthing and Bognor services was completed at Eastleigh and delivered early in 1926. This brought the total number of Ironclads to 154, 114 of which

had entered traffic after the grouping. If you add the 72 SR built Thanets and the 51 vehicles of the second tranche of Contractor and Eastleigh built Continentals together, it reveals that the Southern managed to put in to traffic an impressive 237 stop-gap corridor carriages in a little over two years.

(The author gratefully acknowledges the informative works of Mike King, David Gould, G Weddell, G T Moody and Phil Coutanche in compiling the sections on rolling stock above.)

In Part 5 - Changing Times I will continue the story of the Southern's momentous progress over the first few years of its existence and also take a look at the some of the company's other less obvious interests. I intend to continue the story of rolling stock development with the introduction of new Maunsell stock on all three divisions. The motive power side was also developing new and improved designs to cope with the demand for more power at the head of the train. My thanks go to Nick Hall for the loan of original documentation connected with the signalling at Charing Cross, Cannon Street, London Bridge and North Kent East. Thanks are also owed to David Brown for confirming some of the more obscure signalling details, and to Martin Stone for his patience in checking through the draft manuscript.

Waterloo showing SR built "Ironclad" 4-compartment brake 3rd No.3194, which was formed in Portsmouth Line set 439, about to leave behind S15 No. 847. (Note the MT (for Main Through) showing in the route indicator.) Some of Maunsell S15's were regular performers on Portsmouth workings prior to the full introduction of electric traction. No. 847 was new in December 1936, thus dating the picture to after that date. (There is a picture of No. 847 on p140 of LSWR Locomotives Urie Classes' by D L Bradley, working a Portsmouth line train at Bedhampton in June 1937. The loco went to Exmouth Junction in mid 1937 presumably on the introduction of full electric services on 4 July 1937, so the picture is most probably between these two dates.)
Frank Foote / Mike King collection

PARAFFIN TO COAL

(Via Andover and Salisbury)

(or to be more accurate: from Lamp Lad, Andover, to Fireman at Salisbury)

The Memories of A Happy Man

Peter Brown

Your editor craves the readers indulgence over what is an overdue account of the memories of Peter Brown. Promised originally for Issue No 16, there were cries of disbelief in the office when the computer file in which the notes had been stored was found to be corrupted. A necessary wait then to the current issue, aided by the kind understanding of Peter who was only too willing to recount his tales again.

Peter started on the railway over 65 years ago, as a Lamp Lad at Andover Junction station. Slightly unusually he had no relatives already in the employ of 'the company' but despite this was interviewed and appointed by Mr Hayward, the Andover station master. Andover boasted two 'lamp boys' - as Peter referred to them, one, who would teach Peter the job was Vic Cronin, the other had been Bernard White, but he was waiting to leave Andover to start as a cleaner 'with the loco at Eastleigh' and it was Bernard's position that was being taken over by Peter.

Being a lamp lad / boy might have seemed a menial task but it was nevertheless an essential role, without illumination in the signals drivers would not be aware of their indication at night and so to avoid the wrath of signalman, drivers and station master there was care taken to see that what were invariably 7-day lamps did in fact last the requisite 7-day period.

Vic and Peter worked opposite each other on either early or late shift. When I asked Peter what occurred when one or other might have been absent, he paused for a moment before recounting, 'I think we covered for each other'. This would also be the only time during our discussions when he was unsure of a fact, all others immediately recounted from a sharp and vivid memory, Peter never having kept notes or a diary - although he admits now he wishes he had. (This wonderful memory was apparent later in our discussion when referring to specific locomotives, men he worked with, the turns and train times. He would recall these instantly, whilst at the same time his hand would be going out as if operating the injector, brake, regulator or whatever - each clearly having been handled with just the right amount of effort for the occasion.)

But to return to Andover. The daily routine saw a regular 'round' of work cleaning, refilling and polishing the signal lamps both in the station area as well as over a wider area. Within the station area for example there were some 50 signal lamps to attend, which included ground signals, as well as on the up-main a five-arm bracket controlling access from the main line to either the up-through or up-local as well as the branch (the former MSWJ) which ran as a single line from Red Post and allowed trains from Weyhill to the up-local, branch platform, or branch siding. In addition to the station, the lamps west of Andover at Red Post Junction and those to the east, the Enham Intermediate signals, were similarly attended to. Andover Town however was not his responsibility, this location having its own lamp-man, although the lads did look after the lamps in the home signals leading from the branch into the bay and on to the main line.

It was at Enham, some two miles east of Andover that Peter had one particular experience, which when recounting, he spoke of with a wry smile. The practice was firstly to clean and polish one fresh lamp at Andover itself and then carry this out to the down-distant, here replacing the old lamp with the new. The old lamp was then taken to the nearby lamp-hut, where it in turn was cleaned, refilled and polished and then put in the up-distant distant. The practice was similarly repeated with another rejuvenated lamp intended for the Enham Intermediate home-signal, over 4,000 yards from Andover itself. On the occasion in question Peter had attended to the lamp and was walking with it

S15 No. 30499 with milk near Folly Bridge, Andover.   *Rod Hoyle*

towards the signal when a shout from a ganger walking to-wards him in the opposing direction made him look around. The lamp hut he had just left was on fire. To be fair the building was little more than an arrangement of wooden sleepers which over the years had also become liberally soaked in paraffin. Whatever explanation was arrived at by

offialdom must have satisfied hierarchy as Peter heard no more about it. He did regret though the loss of two particular lamps which also contained electrical repeaters.

In the opposite direction the lads would attend Red Post Junction weekly. Here there were also some lamps that were electrically repeated whilst there was another 'intermediate' lamp hut where paraffin, spare lamps, wicks, burners and cleaning equipment was stored. This one was fortunate in escaping the pyrotechnic experience of its cousin.

I asked Peter how supplies of paraffin etc were delivered and he recounted they would arrive , he thought from Eastleigh, he recalled in 5-gallon drums (although perhaps more likely this was initially in 45 gallon capacity.) To visit Red Post in the morning the practice was to cadge a lift on the goods which left Andover for Ludgershall at 8.15 am. The drum of paraffin would be left with the guard although Peter would invariably try and ride on the engine. On both this and subsequent occasions, his requests were rarely refused and it thus becomes easy to see how his interest in footplate work commenced. He would then be dropped off in the vicinity of Red Post Junction but after completing his tasks would invariably have to walk back.

Peter recalled it was essential to let a replenished lamp 'settle'. Failure to do so could result in it smoking or going out. Either would mean a call from the signalman to attend, he in turn having been alerted by a train crew. Such was the case late one evening when Peter received a call that the up distant for Red Post had been reported as 'out'. This was some two miles from Andover station whilst Peter's protestations that his father would not like him venturing out on his own at night fell on deaf ears.

Between the two boys, work on the lamps was usually completed before the end of the late shift at 10.00 pm, and meaning the rest of the time would be spent on the platform 'portering'. There was though also responsibility for tail lamps, Andover, like most other intermediate stations, keeping a stock of these for use as required. Peter recalled they were several of different types and whilst a Southern man through and through was also willing to admit the Western lamps were of a superior standard. (He recounted later some of the locomen were not the kindest to their engine head-lamps putting these out by literally knocking the lamp hard on to the ground rather than the simple expedient of opening the case and blowing it out. Apparently it was common for train tail lamps to need replacing, care being taken to exchange a Western / Southern lamp for one of similar type.)

Portering was clearly not favoured by Peter, one evening experience coming to mind which involved milk churns. The arrangement was for an up milk service to stop at Andover in the process of which two 15 gallon churns would be dropped off for the local milkman. Every night this milkman would be regularly waiting, except on this one, rare, occasion. So Peter, having taken the churns off the van naturally expected to see the milkman by the time they were both on the platform. But the milkman was not there, nor had he arrived by the time they were placed on the porter's barrow, or by the time Peter had started to wheel this towards the slope leading to the subway that linked the main

platform. The next stage was to trundle the trolley down the slope which he did, but Peter's experience with what was weighty load were clearly not as good as the milkman's, as the barrow ran away colliding with the end wall emptying the churns in the process - of course just at the same moment the milkman appeared around the corner of the subway. Then there was the incident with the box of live eels. These had been collected from the river Test near Stockbridge and were being transported in an open box to Andover ready to be transferred to another train to reach their destination. They never ventured past Andover, the box accidentally dropped with the eels escaping down the various drains and watercourses in the area to wriggle (live) another day.

Peter's change towards loco work came about partly because of a trip west on the footplate one evening. It was just after 9.00 pm and the 9.08 pm for Salisbury was waiting at the down platform. Peter was due to finish at 10.00 pm and there was little to do between that time and now. He asked the driver, Charlie Letchford of Nine Elms, if he could ride with him and the request was quickly granted. At Salisbury Charlie came off, his return working being the Sidmouth milk fortunately due to stop at Andover on its way up to London. Arriving back at Andover, Charlie advised Peter to alight on the offside so as not to be seen by the platform staff. This Peter did, taking care to miss a light engine which was approaching 'wrong-line' on the up-through ready to detach two vans from the rear. Arriving home Peter had to explain his later than expected arrival but that was noting to the words he received from Charlie the next night when he again asked to ride with him Charlie had seen him get off and then seen the engine pass by, but he had not seen Peter afterwards, neither it appears had Charlie's fireman. The result was sleepless night for Charlie worrying that Peter had been knocked over.

The incident passed and encouraged by what were becoming regular footplate trips with Charlie, and others, Peter applied for a transfer 'to the Loco'. This was refused by the station master, Charlie's advice to Peter when imparting this sad news being simple, '...tell his you will resign if he will not let you transfer.' Such words did the trick and on 23 September 1946, exactly a year after starting at Andover, Peter reported for duty as cleaner at Salisbury shed. At the time the man in charge as shed-master was Mr Shears, although Peter did not recall being interviewed by him at any stage.

Little time was spent cleaning, as with a then acute shortage of firemen there was some urgency to get cleaners capable of footplate work. Consequently after just a few weeks he was put with Wally Golton and Len Abbott, a Salisbury disposal crew whose task included meeting engines upon arrival at Salisbury and taking these to the shed for servicing. He recalls the very first of these was a 'D15' which had arrived on a Portsmouth via Eastleigh working.

Peter Brown on the footplate of No 412 at Salisbury in 1947. This engine was delivered new to Salisbury in 1904 and had the dubious distinction of being one of the engines involved in the Salisbury disaster two years later. As can be seen, it was repaired and lasted until 1951.

The 'junior' was given the unenviable but essential task of emptying the smoke box and then going underneath to rake out the ash pan. The next task was to deal with the engine off the 12.50 from Waterloo, recalled as No. 453. Just a week was spent on this work before it was out as a junior fireman on the East Yard shunter. (Peter recalled there were five regular shunting jobs from Salisbury, East Yard shunter, East Yard passenger shunter, West Yard shunter, West Yard passenger shunter, and shunter Western side. He also recalled working No. 361 over the Market House branch from Salisbury. This line saw little traffic, perhaps only once or twice a week and then usually only with a wagon or two of corn.) Later on, another line over which he worked was that from Salisbury through Downton to West Moors and Wimborne. Some of his drivers on this, seemingly intent on exchanging tablets at Breamore as fast as they could - to such an extent that the signalman there threatened to refuse to have a tablet for them next time if they repeated this behaviour. There was also the 'Sprat and Winkle' south from Andover, although in steam days the only turn Salisbury men had over this was with one through freight train.

What might be expected to happen next was a gradual and slow rise through the various turns gaining experience in the process. Officially this was still the case although the opportunity also existed for an occasional temporary move to cover an unexpected vacancy. Such was the case one day when a main line fireman failed to turn up for duty. The driver concerned was a Salisbury man, Ted Bolt, who was then normally working with fireman Ronnie Norris. Ted was due to take a main line service to Waterloo but who instead readily accepted Peter on the turn. (Unbeknown to offialdom Peter had ridden with Ted before and it was on occasions such as this that Peter had been taught the art of firing a moving train. This was also helped by Peter riding between work at Salisbury and his home station of Andover on the footplate whenever possible.) The service was the 6.45 am all stations to Woking thence fast to Waterloo, not perhaps the fastest but still an exacting duty for a 'rookie' on No 448 with 10 bogies. The return was easy, on the cushions of the 'ACE'. The trip was accomplished without undue difficulty although Peter did admit he was somewhat tired as a result. Having proved himself to Ted in that way, word quickly spread and he was often sought after to cover similar vacancies when they arose. (Peter also recounted the characters of some of the men he worked with, such as Ted Bolt. Ted for example backing the winning horse in the 1949 Grand National. 'Russian Hero', a 66-1 outsider which result in a nice little return on a 6d each way bet.)

But that is not to think all were easy trips, another occasion was with a 'Paddlebox' on a freight to Eastleigh, recalled as not an easy journey at all, not helped by the engine having a flat firebed but also with no words of encouragement or assistance from that particular driver. (Some drivers would say little if anything all day, finishing with a 'see you tomorrow then' as they went home.) Then there was the occasion one very cold winter's day he was called upon to pair up with a driver and take a train of coke from Salisbury to Templecombe with No. 745. As Peter recounted , 'I had terrible trouble, not helped by having an engine that by the size of its wheels was totally unsuitable for the type of work - I struggled for steam most of the way'. To make matters worse, upon arrival they were directed to return tender-first to Salisbury. (This story has a postscript, as No. 745 also happened to be the engine of the train that took Peter home from work the same day - and of course it was blowing off steam without difficulty.)

Peter recounted working the branch to Amesbury and Bulford although he never went beyond the latter to Bulford Camp. 'Going was easy, it was the coming back that was difficult. Leaving Amesbury it was a hard pull all the way to Newton Tony and we were very often short of steam even with just two coaches.' Peter explained further that this was with an M7 on a push-pull working whilst being on his own on the footplate he had to be careful to make sure he saw when the driver at the other end shut the regulator. Failure to do so could result in a '14-foot sheet of flame.......'.

This prompted me to ask the question how did he rate particular types of engine he worked upon. At the top of the list were the 'King Arthur' and rebuilt 'Bulleid' types. This was followed by the 'T9' and 'D15' with a 'Remembrance' as '50/50'. Disliked were, not surprisingly the 'Paddlebox' but also the '330' and '700' types. (We then discussed the various 'Western' types that became familiar to Peter after the two sheds and workings were combined, the results were perhaps slightly surprising.....)

I also asked Peter if he had any experience of the original 'Bulleid' 'Merchant Navy' type and he admitted he had. He now started to talk about how some locomen (regretfully he said the majority) who were on the railway only as a job with little care for what they did or how they used the engines. This was illustrated with an unspecified trip on a 'Merchant' with an unnamed driver. Peter freely admitted the reverser on these engines would creep, whilst some of the drivers did not seem to bother to look where it had reached. Consequently with the engine perhaps now at 40% cut-off instead of the desired 25% the amount of coal being burnt and water used was considerable. The fire would also become white hot. Come the time the next stopping place was reached, it seemed as if a number of these drivers did not care to slow the train properly either: they would approach the station, feel they were not stopping and in panic apply the brakes fully: the result on the engine was the water running forward and the safety valves lifting, '280 lbs from both valves all over the place' was how Peter described it. He also recounted how under the same circumstances he had seen drivers put the engine in reverse and open the regulator....'what a way to treat an engine' he exclaimed.

As the years progressed so did Peter's regular turns on the main line. These included having a regular driver as well as gaining experience with any number of different men. One of these was 'Doc', a character recalled by Peter as 'liking his drink' with Friday being the worst time when he had just been paid. Many a time Doc had admitted to

Peter he had better do the driving whilst Doc busied himself on the shovel - quiet well apparently despite his condition. They worked in this fashion on a number of occasions, including one where they had the rebuilt No. 35028 and left Salisbury six minutes late yet were right-time at Waterloo. (Peter recounted one of these times when after arrival they went to Nine Elms and thence to what he described as the 'dirty, filthy excuse of a cabin at Nine Elms' for their break. 'Doc's' behaviour was evidently known to his wife as well for on opening his sandwiches he was presented with the sight of a pork-chop between two slices of bread - something about having spent all his time in the pub before work rather than going home for his lunch before duty. 'Mrs Doc' had therefore presented his dinner in this way, except this was no use to Doc for he was a man without teeth. The 'pork chop sandwich' was unceremoniously thrown across the cabin.

At Salisbury they would sometimes relieve on a London-bound turn where six minutes was allowed at Salisbury for a crew change, refilling the tender and pushing coal forward - the engine having already worked up from Exeter. To assist the new fireman another man was allocated, officially to pull coal forward, but as Peter recounted, 'they rarely worked hard, after all we would be gone in six minutes, after which it was not their problem'.

Listening to Peter he was justifiably proud also of some of his turns. Like the time they had No. 35018 'fresh from a short back and sides' (an expression I learnt which meant after the engine had received an intermediate overhaul, rather than the tightness associated with a 'full works' job). For whatever reason the driver did not want to drive, but even with '13 on' and another late departure they were still right time at Waterloo. Later, as a passed-man, Peter would relieve main line drivers at Salisbury receiving a scowl from the departing driver witnessing a young man about to take his seat. (I did ask Peter if any of the drivers he worked with ever spoke about their own early days. Peter recounted they did not, but now of course wished he had asked them.)

In his career Peter was involved in one serious incident which could have had terrible consequences. The duty was with No. 858 taking just three coaches and a van on a stopping service from Waterloo to Salisbury. This turn involved relief in the platform at which point No. 858 was already blowing off furiously. There was no sign of water in the glass but they were assured by the crew it was there and somewhere out of sight above the top nut. Peter's driver, Fred Johnson was thus unconcerned. Even so Peter decided to play safe, probably what saved his life, for with his now considerable footplate experience he set the injector to feed about the same amount of water into the boiler as he estimated they were using. As such they proceeded to Basingstoke where they were pulled forward and then set back into the down bay (formerly the platform also used by Alton

Salisbury fireman: D. Parsons (left), an un-named Nine Elms driver, and Salisbury driver, 'Doc' Allen.

trains). After the departure of a Bournemouth line service they followed on to Worting and it was at the next station, Oakley, that disaster occurred. The fusible plugs melted, depositing what was left of the boiler contents into the firebox although fortunately at the time with the firebox doors closed. They were eventually hauled to Salisbury by a '700' whilst at the subsequent enquiry it was found that the various waterways to and from the gauge glass were blocked with scale and it would not have been possible to obtain a true reading.

This led Peter to start talking about his times on the 'Western' from Salisbury and which came about following a BR amalgamation of the two sheds and their work. Even so, Western engines continued to work over Western lines. To the Southern men there was less upheaval but to the Western men, forced now to clean their own fires, ashpans and smokeboxes it was a culture shock. Asked about the relative merits of WR locomotives, Peter freely admitted he liked the 'Hall', 'Grange' and 'Manor' type as well as the various 'Prairie', 'Pannier' and '72xx'. He was less complimentary about the 'Castle' saying, '...we only got them after they had been thrashed on the Bristolian and had been downgraded on to the Cardiff / Bristol - Portsmouth trains. We did not need them, they were a lot of hard work, the others could it the job just as well'. He was also very complimentary about the 'Pannier tanks'. (Better not say any more about that in a Southern magazine!)

Before rationalisation it was also a common practice if two trains left Salisbury simultaneously westbound for a race to develop. One would be on the Southern line, the other destined for the Western and Westbury. All good-natured fun. Peter also found himself working on Western engines after their duties had been amalgamated. One of these included a turn to Bristol and which on the return, found Peter wanting to put some more coal on the fire near Wishford. He was stopped by the driver, who announced 'there is plenty in there already'; which Peter found a rather strange remark especially as his driver had not looked in the firebox once. Even so he obeyed. Matters might have been fine except they were delayed by signals and when the driver went to blow off the brakes steam had dropped and to cap it all the fire had gone out. Needless to say Peter got the blame, the Salisbury loco inspector seemingly siding with the driver's version of events. Peter recounts he felt it best to bite his tongue as it would be that same inspector who would shortly hopefully be passing his for driving.

Whilst at Salisbury the prestige 'ACE' duty was given to Salisbury men, one of the reasons for this being better timekeeping. In the up direction, the crew would book on at 1.44 pm and after reading any notices were allowed 15 minutes walking time to the station. The actual service was due at 2.09 with departure 2.15 pm. Peter would again talk of ensuring the fireman was ready, 'trouble was they never really cleaned out the tenders properly', explaining that as time passed so an accumulation of dross and muck would accumulate right at the bottom of the tender which, with water being added all the time to damp down the dust, could result in a deep layer of rubbish on top of which fresh coal was continually being added. The quality of coal available was also mentioned, 'Yorkshire hard would burn fast -

'PARAFFIN TO COAL: via ANDOVER and SALISBURY'

like paper, Welsh took a while to get going'.

We also spoke of the standard types. 'The 75's and 76's were good, but I did not like the 73's - all rattles and draughts'. (He was only on '9F once, with a petrol train from Fawley routed via Westbury. 'As we went down the bank from Warminster the driver thought he was not going to stop, so he put the lot in.......I thought they were going to all pile up behind us.'

Fifteen years at Salisbury saw promotion and with it a move to Fratton where Peter would remain for the rest of his driving career. At first this was on both steam and diesel, the steam turns taking in trips to Waterloo, Brighton and some of the local lines, such as Gosport. I asked him if he worked to Hayling and received the following response, ' I managed to avoid that....'. When pushed why he explained, 'having been used to the big ones I could not take to those little Rooters' (meaning the 'Terriers') He continued, 'we did take one to Littlehampton once for shunting, that was bad enough'. (Peter also mentioned eye-sight, he has worn glasses for many years and admitted he was fortunate in transferring when he did as a steam man was not permitted to wear glasses whilst a diesel / electric man could. 'It was terrible to see those old steam men pushing a broom round the shed labouring where they could not be on the footplate any more.')

Diesel work from Fratton included regular driving back to Andover via Stockbridge whilst later Peter was put into the 'dual-link' meaning he could also work electric stock. This was in the mid-1960s, the time also they were working on the abolition of steam with London Transport electric trains for the Isle of Wight. 'We were all taken up to London to see the new electric trains, looked like they had been in store for years, filthy they were. I said they will never get them cleaned up and was told wait and see. Well, after they were transferred some of us were sent over the Island sometimes to cover', (I asked Peter if that meant he had to do route learning first from Ryde, but he replied all that was left there was really a siding down to Shanklin.). 'Trouble was they never did clear out all that rubbish, when you braked the rattling would dislodge hundreds of bugs from every crevice every time - we used to carry a can of bug spray in the cab with us'. 'The Inspector at Pier Head used to say those Fratton men would arrive much too fast and that one day he expected to see the front coach in the Solent. He never did. But I did put a Western DMU through the end wall at Salisbury shed once.......'. (Perhaps on both occasions Peter had been thinking back to his days on the 'ACE'!)

(We would like to thank Eric Hobbs for his suggestion that a chat with Peter would be worthwhile, how right he was.)

Right - Peter Brown in his new guise, covering relief on the Isle of Wight. (The can of 'bug spray' will no doubt be close at hand.)

Overleaf - 'Twilight at Furzebrook (narrow-gauge line)'. Edward Griffiths, courtesy Carole Griffiths.

Issue No 18 of *THE SOUTHERN WAY* (ISBN 978-1-906419-78-3) should be available in April 2012 at £12.95

To receive your copy the moment it is released, order in advance from your usual supplier, or direct from the publisher:

Kevin Robertson (Noodle Books) PO Box 279, Corhampton, SOUTHAMPTON, SO32 3ZX

Tel 01489 877880 www.noodlebooks.co.uk